"A unique and precious mingling of disciplines, nourished by multilingual sources, this manual will help students and professionals in culture management to better comprehend what cultural capital and cultural capitalism are. Based upon a critical analysis, it restitutes synthetically the main social and aesthetic revolutions of the last century."

François Ruegg, *Professor Emeritus, Universities of Fribourg and Bucharest*

"This exciting new course book on *Cultural Capital and Creative Communication* is a timely and useful addition to the field for scholars and students alike. Oana Șerban provides a wide-ranging and stimulating epistemic overview of the interrelated concepts of cultural capital, capital, and art, focusing on the work of key thinkers evolving in the political, intellectual and artistic context of 20th-century Europe."

Alex Frame, *Associate Professor, University of Burgundy*

"This welcomed book, authored by Oana Șerban, has the merit of being both a manual in the usual sense of the term, that of a useful pedagogical tool for students to approach an extremely complex field of our cultural reality (and not only), but also a scientific, passionate investigation of the current state of the art in this domain. The openings, temptations and risks of the theoretical approach that will inevitably captivate the reader appear as soon as we notice that we deal with a book that evaluates the dynamics of cultural capital, and the manner, particularly dramatic and actual, of entangling with the economic and the cultural spheres in all layers of our society and life. About the balance, more or less successful, but inevitable today, between cultural capital and the culture of capital, you will find more in the pages of this volume."

Viorel Vizureanu, *Professor, University of Bucharest*

Cultural Capital and Creative Communication

Inspired by Bourdieu's thought, this book explores the notion of cultural capital, offering insights into its various definitions, its evolution and the critical theories that engage with it.

Designed for use by students and teachers, it addresses the limitations and expansion of Bourdieu's theory of capital and power, considering the relationship between cultural, social and human capital, the distinctions between capital and capitalism, and the conflicts that exist among theories that have emerged in response to – or can be brought to bear on – Bourdieu's work. Engaging with the thought of Max Weber, Fernand Braudel, Daniel Bell, Herbert Marcuse, Jean Baudrillard, Theodor Adorno, Max Horkheimer and Gilles Lipovetsky, *Cultural Capital and Creative Communication* represents the first book to develop a field of research and study that is devoted to cultural capital.

Richly illustrated with empirical examples and offering assessment exercises, it will appeal not only to scholars and students of sociology, philosophy and social theory, but also to corporate communities who seek to develop training modules on the increase of their cultural capital.

Oana Şerban teaches Modern Philosophy and Aesthetics at the University of Bucharest, Romania, as titular professor of the Department of Practical Philosophy and History of Philosophy and of the UNESCO Chair in Interculturality, Good Governance and Sustainable Development. She is the Executive Director of CCIIF – The Research Center for the History and Circulation of Philosophical Ideas (UB). She has authored *Artistic Capitalism* (2016) and *After Thomas Kuhn. The Structure of Aesthetic Revolutions* (2022) and co-edited different volumes of philosophy, culture and aesthetics. Around 30 academic articles and studies reflect her interest in the following main areas of expertise: Aesthetics, Modern and Political Philosophy, History of Philosophy, Biopolitics, History of Art, Cultural Heritage. Currently, she is exploring the biopolitical potential of modern art, in her latest study, published in the volume *Philosophy and Film: Bridging Divides* (ed. Christina Rawls, Diana Neiva, Steven Gouveia) (Routledge, 2019).

Routledge Studies in Social and Political Thought

This series explores core issues in political philosophy and social theory. Addressing theoretical subjects of both historical and contemporary relevance, the series has broad appeal across the social sciences. Contributions include new studies of major thinkers, key debates and critical concepts.

Cultural Capital and Creative Communication

(Anti-)Modern and (Non-)Eurocentric Perspectives

Oana Șerban

Routledge
Taylor & Francis Group

LONDON AND NEW YORK

First published 2023
by Routledge
4 Park Square, Milton Park, Abingdon, Oxon OX14 4RN

and by Routledge
605 Third Avenue, New York, NY 10158

Routledge is an imprint of the Taylor & Francis Group, an informa business

© 2023 Oana Şerban

The right of Oana Şerban to be identified as author of this work has been asserted in accordance with sections 77 and 78 of the Copyright, Designs and Patents Act 1988.

British Library Cataloguing-in-Publication Data
A catalogue record for this book is available from the British Library

Library of Congress Cataloging-in-Publication Data
Names: Şerban, Oana, 1991- author.
Title: Cultural capital and creative communication : (anti)modern and (non)eurocentric perspective / Oana Şerban.
Description: Milton Park, Abingdon, Oxon ; New York, NY : Routledge, 2023. | Includes bibliographical references and index.
Identifiers: LCCN 2022045472 (print) | LCCN 2022045473 (ebook) | ISBN 9781032360133 (hardback) | ISBN 9781032360140 (paperback) | ISBN 9781003329855 (ebook)
Subjects: LCSH: Social capital (Sociology) | Community life.
Classification: LCC HM708 .S47 2023 (print) | LCC HM708 (ebook) | DDC 302--dc23/eng/20220927
LC record available at https://lccn.loc.gov/2022045472
LC ebook record available at https://lccn.loc.gov/2022045473

ISBN: 978-1-032-36013-3 (hbk)
ISBN: 978-1-032-36014-0 (pbk)
ISBN: 978-1-003-32985-5 (ebk)

DOI: 10.4324/9781003329855

Typeset in Times New Roman
by SPi Technologies India Pvt Ltd (Straive)

Contents

Figures

Introduction

This book offers multiple insights into the operational definitions, taxonomy, evolutions and critical theories of cultural capital. Inspired by Bourdieu's theories on the forms of capital, this manual has been designed initially as a manual for the classes and seminars of Cultural Capital and Creative Communication, held for the students from the MA programmes of the UNESCO Chair in Interculturality, Good Governance and Sustainable Development, of the University of Bucharest. In time, this class also became quite a fashionable educational offer for many students of our university from other departments and, therefore, a manual has been conceived, aiming to address: the limits and expansions of Bourdieu's theory on capital and power; the relationship between cultural, social and human capital; the distinctions between capital and capitalism; as well as the major conflict between theories that address differently the (Non-)Eurocentric paternity of capital, and capitalism respectively. Alongside Bourdieu, readers of this book will find interdisciplinary and critical undertakings of Max Weber, Fernand Braudel, Daniel Bell, Herbert Marcuse, Jean Baudrillard, Theodor Adorno, Max Horkheimer and Gilles Lipovetsky.

It is the first manual designed at the heart of philosophy and sociology that aims to develop a recent field of research and study that is devoted to cultural capital. It is a practical title because it reflects the interest not only of academic audiences but also of corporate communities who have the opportunity to secure and increase the growth of their cultural capital, therefore, the manual could also be used for training devoted to such target groups.

When I started to teach Cultural Capital and Creative Communication, I was surprised to discover that my students were divided into being either partisans of a Eurocentric paternity of capitalism, or supporters of the idea that capitalism is not as modern as we might think at first sight. None of them used to perceive capital and capitalism

DOI: 10.4324/9781003329855-1

through the lens of Non-Western Modernity, whereas only a small part of my academic audience used to conceive the real importance of philosophical discussions on capital(-ism) for the consolidation of culture and art.

Therefore, as professor of Modern Philosophy, I started to reconsider their curricula and to propose, to my MA students from the UNESCO chair, a new perspective to focus on and quantify the evolution of cultural capital. I wanted to demystify some prejudgments connected to Marxist philosophy, and to explain why our modernity is sensitive towards individuality and cherishes ideologies related to individualism, and that there is nothing that could support such concepts more than cultural capital.

My objectives first became aggregate around the need to secure their knowledge on cultural capital. I devised a set of methodological tools and indicators that would allow the assessment of cultural capital in different historical periods and societies and teach students to recognise and become critical of the different criteria that lie at the core of understanding taxonomies of cultural capital. Secondary, explanatory models of cultural capital and its related ideologies became a priority for our educational act: the evaluation of the conceptual and historical clash between cultural capital and social capital. Furthermore, the interpretation of knowledge, skills, values, educational practices and social practices that determine forms of cultural capital across different modern societies reflected one of the major curiosities and legitimate interests of my students. I expected them to engage all their skills of hermeneutical analysis and critical thinking: the rest became part of my job. Together, we tested design instruments of creative communication related to different forms of cultural capital. I utilised team work and role distribution for the development of a set of arguments to address a certain paradigm of cultural capital, as well as to predict its evolution to a certain society defined by core values, norms and principles.

This manual is not an instrument of exclusive theoretical knowledge or practical exercises around the philosophical and sociological insights of cultural capital but, as I have said, it is the first that I am aware of in this field. In fact, I designed it in order to satisfy my personal need to offer to our students a handbook that could guide them more easily towards puzzling over the many theories on forms of capital and capitalism.

There are seven main themes concentrated within five content chapters followed by a final evaluation essay proposal. By the end of this manual, students will have gained knowledge about the following:

1 Propaedeutic aspects. Cultural capital: definition, genealogy, taxonomy.
2 Cultural capital as expression of class inequalities: modern trajectories of capitalist societies. Capital vs. capitalism in cultural terms.
3 Cultural capital and social capital. Cultural knowledge, social status and power.
4 Social and economic dynamics of embodied, objectified and institutionalised cultural capital.
5 Cultural capital in terms of critical theory: leftist and rightist theories on the generation, distribution and development of cultural capital.
6 Social vs. human capital: cultural determination.
7 Creative communication: the role of the arts in the sustainable development of society and cultural capital.

Therefore, this manual is not an infallible instrument, but its major function is to acquaint both academic and corporate audiences, through 28 hours of a modular class, with the genealogy, evolution and challenges of cultural capital and creative communication. Hopefully, formal education on this topic will inspire more exertions, and soon the academic environment could become increasingly useful in shaping and branding forms of cultural capital for private entities and actors, as we live in an age when university traditions and business communities need a larger sense of cohesion and cooperation.

1 Propaedeutic Aspects

Cultural Capital and Its Familiarity with the Legitimate Culture Within a Society

1.1 Definition, Genealogy and Taxonomy

A cross-domain definition, at the borders of philosophy, sociology and critical theory, recommends cultural capital as a cluster of social assets that an individual has, and uses, in order to promote social mobility and communication in a hierarchical, stratified community. Such social assets are conceived as a set of practices, beliefs, principles and values that are formed and developed within a certain community: educational practices and traditions, a certain communicative rationality, fashion styles and cultural trends, that become responsible for the development of the so-called cultural capital.

This is a relational notion that is highly dependent on the social dynamics of individuals within and between social classes. As with economic capital, which relies on the material relation with an economic system, similarly, cultural capital is conceived as a social relation with a cultural system of exchange, composed by *symbolic goods*, which can be understood as corps of knowledge, discourses, art objects and cultural practices among others. However, a system that allows individuals to exchange cultural goods is one that assigns them social status and power.

Debates on cultural capital are quite recent and inspired by educational theories that seek to explain the influence of educational systems and practices on the social performance of individuals outside their academic environment. The most powerful tradition on this topic is the French one, initiated and represented by Pierre Bourdieu.

1.2 The Forms of Capital: Pierre Bourdieu

The social world is accumulated history, argues Bourdieu in the opening of his essay (1986). The Marxist roots of capital (see Marx &

DOI: 10.4324/9781003329855-2

Engels 1990) as a form of accumulated labour inspired Bourdieu's theory that distinguishes, at a first glance, between *material* or *incorporated / embodied forms of capital* and *immaterial* or *symbolic forms of capital*. Both are a source of social energy for the individuals who appropriate them on a private basis of use. In short, capital describes a form of "living labour" which has two major and simultaneous implementations:

1 As *vis insita*, "a force inscribed in objective or subjective structures" (Bourdieu 1986, p. 46).
2 As *lex insita*, "the principle underlying the immanent regularities of the social world" (Bourdieu 1986, p. 46).

There is nothing like chances or indeterminable conditions for tracking the evolution of economy and society. If a roulette game is exclusively focused on the opportunities that an individual has to win a significant amount of money instantly, in terms of fair competition for accumulation, in economy and society the force of prediction is applicable and "sustainable" (Throsby 1995, p. 199). Therefore, there are mechanisms through which capital, in its objectified forms, can be evaluated in its capacity to reflect material accumulation in large units of time. In fact, as Bourdieu explains, capital has the capacity "to produce profits and to reproduce itself in identical or expanded form, (...) is a force inscribed in the objectivity of things so that everything is not equally possible or impossible" (1986, p. 46). As a consequence, Bourdieu considers that:

1 Nobody can understand the construction of the social world until all forms of capital are introduced. Privileging economic capital is a trap.
2 All forms of capital are accumulated in time, not instantly, but whenever it comes about the distribution of different forms of capital at a certain moment of time, every single form of capital represents "the immanent structure of the social world, i.e. the set of constraints, inscribed in the very reality of that world, which govern its functioning in a durable way, determining the chances of success for practices"

(1986, p. 46)

A hidden premise of Bourdieu's argument, at this level, is that capital, in all its subsequent forms, represents a historical necessity, which emerges from a certain historical situation of a particular community in which that form of considered capital appeared and expanded.

Economic forms of capital are related to *self-interested* systems, given the exigencies of mercantile exchange to which they subscribe, but cultural forms of capital, as well as social ones, are related to noneconomic systems of exchange, consequently recognised as *disinterested*. Bourdieu adds, in this regard, that these classes are related: interestedness and disinterestedness are counterparts; therefore, each material object has a cultural or spiritual finality, and vice versa. The most wide-spread prejudgment is that economic science exclusively tracks the material aspects of mercantile relationships neglecting the practices behind them. A more holistic approach is required: Bourdieu seeks a "general science of the economy practices," that adds values, principles, emotions, behaviours and norms to the entire cluster of embodied forms of capital: "private property, profit, wage labour" (1986, p. 47).

Bourdieu identifies three types of capital which are historically co-dependent and can be tracked by some common traits, such as the capacity to be convertible into material / symbolic contents, and to be institutionalised, in certain conditions (see also Figure 1.1).

Bourdieu explains that his theory on cultural capital as a mixture of three correlated forms of *embodied, objectified* and *institutionalised* capital, is not designed in order to produce a forced theoretical axiomatisation. His argument lies on an Aristotelian premise, which invokes the success or the failure of individuals as a direct consequence of their natural dispositions or capacities. Educational interrogations inspired Bourdieu's research on cultural capital, addressing the causes that determine "unequal scholastic achievement of children originating from different social classes and class fractions," and what measures should be adopted in order to control "the distribution of cultural capital between the classes and class fractions" (1986, p. 17). First, Bourdieu proposes the following distinctions between the states of cultural capital (see Figure 1.2).

Second, Bourdieu observes that historically, people tend to pursue a direct correlation between the rate of investment in education and the rates of profit on educational investment, mainly considered as monetary expressions, convertible into material goods. The transfer of cultural capital in terms of education is highly neglected by the most popular approaches of economists since these focus exclusively on developing scholastic investment strategies rather than determining the optimal conditions of the so-called "domestic transmission of cultural capital."

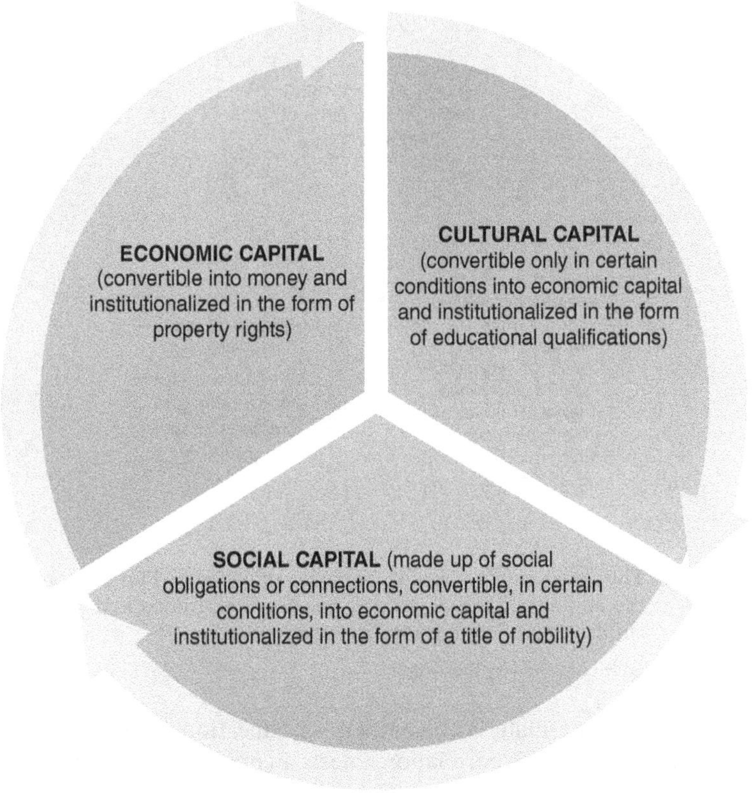

Figure 1.1 The three types of capital according to Pierre Bourdieu: *economic, cultural* and *social capital*, with their particularities related to conversion capacities.

Photograph/table conceived by the author.

Problem (1): Cultural capital has never been tracked as a relationship between academic ability and academic investment.

Following Beker, Bourdieu assumes that there are no sustainable theories that analyse the viability of the relationship between academic ability and academic investment, revealing that "experts are unaware that ability or talent is itself the product of an investment of time and cultural capital." Natural dispositions of individuals must be correlated with developed, hence, artificial dispositions, that emerge from a certain *habitus*, which needs practice in time and accordingly with a proper finality.

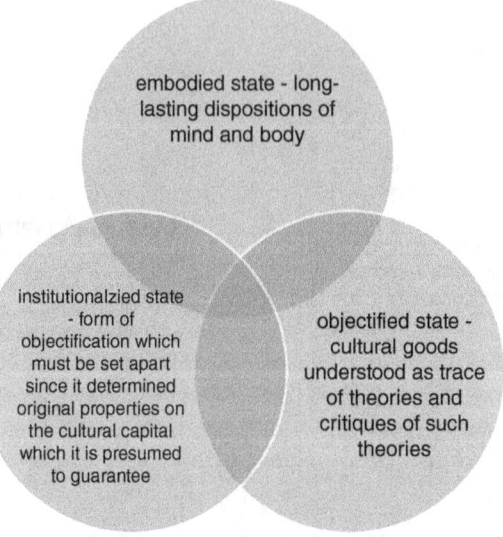

Figure 1.2 The taxonomy of cultural capital, as provided by Pierre Bourdieu: the embodied, the objectified and the institutionalised states of cultural capital, alongside their descriptions.

Photograph/table conceived by the author.

Problem (2): Any material investment in education comes out as a social profit and this correlation reflects an operational sense of cultural capital.

Bourdieu argues that societies tend to transmit cultural capital hereditarily but, since educational systems contribute to the reproduction of the social structures, we should pay more attention to the manner in which any form of cultural capital invested by a family comes out as a source for a social profit.

1.2.1 The Embodied Cultural Capital

Embodied cultural capital depends on a material accumulation of cultural capital. This is the basic form of cultural capital from which the entire *Bildung* of the culture arises.

It involves acquisition as work on oneself (education is considered as a self-improvement), with personal costs, developed in time, but integrated into a social context from which emerges a *libido sciendi*, meaning the forms of renunciation, sacrifice and privation that an individual considers in order to aspire and procure knowledge.

To answer the question of how we acquire and explore such a form of cultural capital, we must understand that:

1 The capacities of an individual determine the accumulation of cultural capital.
2 If "natural capacities" (Throsby 1999, p. 3), memories, habits, languages are related to an individual, then all the emergent forms of cultural capital are linked with the individual's biological singularities.
3 As with any natural dispositions, such elements are either inherited (*to patroa*) or acquired (*epikteta*); Bourdieu adapts the Greek juridical distinctions between the forms of properties and the forms of culture.
4 Therefore, it combines "prestige of innate property with the merits of acquisition." Cultural competences are such forms of embodied cultural capital. They appear in the context of a scarcity value and must be distributed into a class-divided society.

1.2.2 The Objectified Cultural Capital

From the perspective of objectified cultural capital, the focus is mainly on cultural properties. Materiality is the main trait of this form of

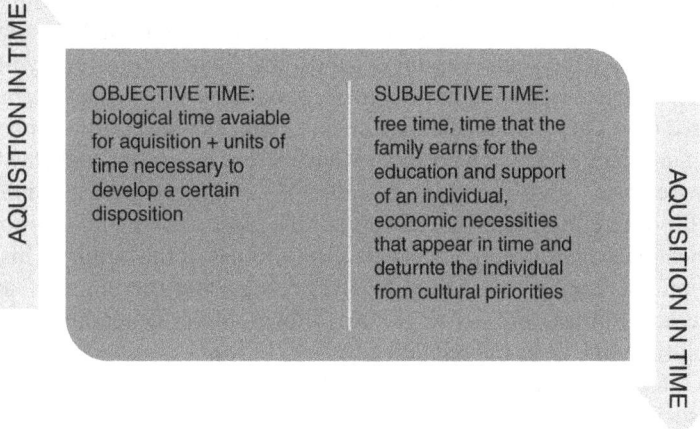

Figure 1.3 The full explanation of the acquisition in time of cultural capital, both in terms of subjective and objective time.

Photograph/table conceived by the author.

cultural capital, and it ensures, by this, the transmission, as well as the conversion towards a form of economic capital. If embodied cultural capital insists on certain conditions for the appearance of a cultural good, objectified cultural capital insists on the conditions in which such a form of cultural good can be consumed (e.g., legal ownership, exposure, and transmission).

1.2.3 The Institutionalised Cultural Capital

Institutionalised expressions of cultural capital relate to roles that individuals develop, given their cultural competences. In education, such elements are conceived as academic qualifications, conventionally obtained and recognised after competitions. In these terms, an institution recognises the cultural capital of its employees. Educational credentials support the development of human and social capital.

1.3 Social Capital: How About Collective Credentials? Production and Reproduction of Social Capital

Institutionalised relationships between individuals as owners of a certain form of cultural capital develop groups or communities. As a consequence, individuals perform symbolic exchanges and contribute to a social capital based on their knowledge, roles, values and behaviours. Social capital is a powerful notion that prescribes the nature of relational networks of social interactions between individuals that engage their forms of capital earning public recognition and mutual acknowledgment. As the social capital expands, the chances to diversify and extend the economic capital increase. Producing social relationships based on dialogue and solidarity involves reproducing cultural or economic capital. Bourdieu considers that there is a sort of "alchemy of consecration" (Bourdieu 1986, p. 250) that constructs, at least symbolically, different types of social capital: the most widespread example, which relies on tradition and societal core values, is the family as institution. Belonging to a group involves recognising the limits of any interaction: trade and marriage have different limits, depending on the exclusivity of the social relationship.

Conservative or liberal visions of the genealogy of groups as forms of social capital transgress modernity as a whole. If, traditionally, families hold the monopoly on different values and commitments (like marriage) through which new members can adhere, nowadays, the logic of the *laissez-faire* dominates the constitution of different forms of social capital. This involves relaxing and diversifying criteria and occasions to expand such structures, through cultural interactions (receptions, festivals and entertainment activities), socialising platforms (neighbourhoods and clubs) and practices (sport clubs and cultural foundations among others). Social capital is reproduced through communication and dynamic exchange of ideas, values and principles. As the investing of personal free time into forms of social cohesion involves time and material comfort, one might argue that higher economic and cultural capital contribute to maximising access to different social groups and opportunities to integrate faster. When someone makes the acquaintance of two persons, it means that each of them increases their social capital. However, groups need representation: there is, without exception, an internal competition to become a leader (*pater familias*, president of a club and so forth). As you become more well-known within a group, you earn opportunities to become one of its representatives. Authority emerges from nobility.

To put this all in a nutshell, the profitability of the labour of accumulating and maintaining social capital rises in proportion to the size of the capital.

1.3.1 Is It Possible to Convert Forms of Cultural Capital?

Bourdieu answers affirmatively: economic capital is the only one that can generate by itself other forms of capital, as long as the process of conversion involves the production of a specific type of power in the field of the future form of the capital. There are two dimensions of the logic of conversion: one which is exclusively economic and stresses that every type of capital emerges from economic capital and is reducible to it, and another one which subscribes to semiologism and insists on the fact that, despite the possibility of reducing any social exchange to communication, individuals still ignore or refuse to accept that their interaction is equally reducible to economics.

The mutual convertibility of the forms of culture represents, in fact, a reliable mechanism through which the reproduction of capital is ensured minimising, in specific conditions, the costs involved in such operation.

1.3.2 Marxism or Post-Marxism?

To the question of whether or not Bourdieu became a Marxist when the capitalist critique was fashionable in the post-war era in France, there is no unanimous agreement between those who tend to answer affirmatively, by understanding cultural capital as an extension of economic capital, and those who tend to deny any powerful continuation of Marxism in Bourdieu's writings, keeping the relationship between them at the level of a theoretical transgression. What seems to be Marxist is rather Bourdieu's perspective on the means of exploiting capital. Social and historical relations of exploitation reveal the grounds for fetishising different forms of capital, mainly the economic one. But Bourdieu is interested in noneconomic goods that perform symbolic, cultural and axiological values. Cultural capital is, somehow, a creative tool that fills a Marxist gap; that of being impractical and relevant in determining the social and cultural interdependencies between individuals during their actions of exchanging economic capital. Moreover, if Marx conceived a political project for his analysis on capital and capitalism (meaning on economic capital and all its related ideological backgrounds and expressions), Bourdieu tracked noncommodity elements as derivative products of a structure. Classes are important for Bourdieu only in terms of social capital: they reflect history in its accumulation, not history in its disruptions and incoherent tensions. For Bourdieu, capital develops multiple forms of power that have a different design from one social field to another, in many noneconomic aspects. Education is the most appropriate platform that historically accumulates and legitimises distinct patterns of social order in which classes are differentiated and maintain the contrasts between them in terms of academic performances and sanctions. In *Distinction* (1987), Bourdieu explains that the economic and cultural forms of capital are determined by class positions and their conditions of existence, which oblige individuals to perform a certain habitus in position-taking in the symbolic space of lifestyles and social dynamics. Hence, Bourdieu is interested in what kind of practices and customs make the bourgeoisie and proletarians behave as they do and not what kind of economic consequences derive from their clash.

Bourdieu deeply reflects on the scarcity of a form of capital in a competitive field, whereas Marx is genuinely committed to analysing the terms of ownership addressed in such a form of capital. Marx considers the relations of production as equivalent to the relations of exploitation, Bourdieu abandons the idea of "equal exchange" (Throsby 1997, p. 7) and seeks for a self-valorising value of a form of capital within a social community.

Therefore, Bourdieu considers that commodities gain their importance not in terms of accumulation or appropriation, but in terms of profitable use, which contradicts the Marxist arguments.

Whereas his critical sociology generally consists in theoretically unmasking the hidden logic of power within cultural fields,

Bourdieu implies that for the economy, where science and native experience coincide, critique consists only in historicizing its already transparent logic

(Desan 2013, p. 334)

Given these trajectories, it would be appropriate to argue that Bourdieu is the author of a theory on cultural capital which lacks capitalism as a field of ideological power. Therefore, his appetite for critical sociology comes from a focused interest in what might be called an economy of practices, not an economy of goods. Bourdieu seeks the general expressions and forms of capital, often emerging from epistemological gaps of historicised critical registers.

Questions: Evaluation

Task 1

Demonstrate comprehension of the presentation of this chapter by answering the following questions:

Q.1 What is Marxist and non-Marxist in Bourdieu's theory on the reproduction of cultural capital?

Q.2 How do we relate cultural capital and habitus? Explain your theoretical position by choosing one concrete example of cultural capital and its related habitus.

Q.3 Is it desirable to combat educational inequalities and, if so, what is the future of applying Bourdieu's theory of cultural capital in addressing better instruments to improve academic performances and minimise educational inequalities?

Task 2

Choose a specific form of cultural capital and explain its production and reproduction mechanisms by illustrating its relationship with a certain form of related social capital. Follow the relationship between cultural capital – values – attitudes – behaviours – rewards – sanctions.

References

Bourdieu, P., 1986, "The Forms of Capital," in J. Richardson (ed.), *Handbook of Theory and Research for the Sociology of Education*, Greenwood, Westport, CT, pp. 241–258.

Bourdieu, P., 1987, *Distinction*, trans. by R. Nice, Harvard University Press, Cambridge, MA.

Desan, M. H., 2013, "Bourdieu, Marx, and Capital: A Critique of the Extension Model," in *Sociological Theory*, Vol. 31, No. 4, pp. 318–342.

Marx, K. & Engel, F., 1990, *Capital. A Critique of Political Economy*, Vol. I, intro. by E. Mandel, trans. by B. Fowkes, Penguin Books, in association with New Left Review, New York.

Throsby, D., 1995, "Culture, Economics and Sustainability," in *Journal of Cultural Economics*, Vol. 19, pp. 199–206.

Throsby, D., 1997, "Sustainability and Culture: Some Theoretical Issues," in *International Journal of Cultural Policy*, Vol. 4, pp. 7–20.

Throsby, D., 1999, "Cultural Capital," in *Journal of Cultural Economics*, Vol. 23, pp. 3–12.

2 Capital and Capitalism
Before and After Cultural Determinations

2.1 Capital and Capitalism: Before and After Cultural Determinations

Capital and capitalism are connected routinely, as if their interdependence is self-evident and implicit. In fact, whenever this conceptual relationship occurs, we should examine the clash between a structure and its ideology. Does capital precede capitalism, historically, ontologically and economically? Are there any social realities that capital-ism, as ideology, tends to explain and that are not objectively trackable only by considering capital, by itself? Is capital an exclusive modern construct, together with its assigned ideological construction, capitalism, or the only thing that betrays a modern reflex is the –ism that follows an ahistorical notion, that of capital? In what follows, we will answer all these critical interrogations from which the cultural contradictions of capitalism, in the formula advanced by Daniel Bell, emerged.

The 19th century became impregnated and conquered by the Marxist economic view. As the material layers of our existence became a primary concern in any attentive examination of social reality, the individual started to conceive of belonging to civilisation as *homo faber*. Progressively, culture was revealed to be a reliable territory for any change, more or less projected as revolution. The historical dynamics of culture has at its core a cultural impulse that societies naturally develop in establishing norms and values for their communitarian identity. These energies that follow up any radical change, not in terms of exclusive material costs, in modernity, open the tradition of the new, as Rosenberg conventionally calls it. It was fostered as a set of beliefs and behaviours that altered canonical, thus archaic or classical, modes of experience, sensation and reflection, based on the Cartesian premise that "good sense is the best shared-out thing in the world" (Descartes 2017, p. 1). If our reason can, by itself, create new norms

DOI: 10.4324/9781003329855-3

for our knowledge, understanding and society, then any cultural construction that follows such a pattern will implicitly abolish the task of reflecting existing social structures and will inspire new ones instead. Novelty represents the fundamental category of the avant-garde as a cultural paradigm specific to modernity. In Bell's opinion (1972, p. 35), one of the first avant-gardists is Saint-Simon, who promotes a cult which can conquer modern civilisation instead of religion or science. But this energy and revisionary power, that artists gained in modernity, weakened once revolutions, conceived as forms of radical change, became institutionalised. From the moment when avant-gardes, as militant forces for the deinstitutionalisation of culture became classicised, socially embodied in different communities and institutions, modernity started to follow new paths for its liberation. Culture has always been reactionary and liberating along modernity: "In effect, 'culture' has been given a blank check, and its primacy in generating social change has been firmly acknowledged" (Bell 1972, p. 13).

Therefore, modernity has been shaped by two forces, one profoundly and genuinely rational, such as economic rationality, through which any human action is rationalised, the other one anti-intellectual, privileging our inferior faculties of thought, such as the imagination and free will, which are at the core of our modern culture. At one point, economy started to work against culture: the bourgeoisie, as a class of well-being, developed a culture highly rejected for its impulsive reactions towards control and dominance. Consequently, social theories began to be "cofounded", as Bell observes, by the new cultural trends. Sorokin's perspective that modern society has a "sensate mentality" that follows empirical roots and technological assessments, thus neglecting and progressively abolishing the possessive culture of the elites, or Weber's considerations that rational forms of thought conquer the cultural production of modern societies, are two examples invoked by Bell in order to stress that culture started to perform a contra-culture. Similarly, art began to develop an anti-art form of sensibility.

2.2 Daniel Bell: The Cultural Contradictions of Capitalism

These changes – the search for new aesthetic experience, the breakup of formal genres, and the detachment of lifestyles from a fixed social base – have become most evident in the last decade, and create the most perplexing problems for social analysis (Bell 1972, p. 14).

Daniel Bell argues that, typically, radical changes have been predictable: they represent changes performed by social groups or communities that adapt to societal variables targeting a strategic position, a systematic interest, or a behavioural finality, which can be considered feasible and achievable in a certain unit of time. Moreover, their fulfilment depends on social attributes (sex, profession, confession, urban-rural location and lifestyle). Modern society is shaped by the relationship between social positions and cultural styles. "Age and education" (1972, p. 15) are relevant discriminators in predicting the cultural behaviour that an individual will embrace at a certain moment, but there is something more important, that suggests the construction of freedom of a social class, and that is the so-called discretionary income. It reflects the amount allocated by individuals for a particular consumption style that goes beyond their education or social role; a sort of permissive context that reveals an important working hypothesis: it is not the occupational base of a class that predicts the social behaviours of its agents, but their cultural tastes and lifestyles. Discretionary income is related to discretionary social behaviour – individuals invest a part of their income in personal experiences and personal desires, that are only partially related to their "somatic body-type constitution, positive or negative experience with parents, experience with peers etc." (Bell 1978, p. 38). If I have problems with my spine I can choose to do swimming or riding. A medical need based on my genetic capital or physical constitution seems to be a factor that can easily determine the variables of my social behaviour associated with leisure time. But, it may be that this is not a priority for me, so I choose to learn chess or play billiards instead, because in my circle of friends, everyone does this and, since our tastes are alike, I will invest my discretionary income in order to satisfy my curiosity and give pleasure and to spend time with my friends.

What Daniel Bell rightfully observes is that any form of dominant culture develops an "adversary culture" and modernity is dominantly composed of such tension. Any change is reducible to the clash between "the dissociation of social location and cultural styles" (Bell 1978, p. 39).

On the one hand, the manner in which societies succeed in generating a creative expression of this correlation is highly important for the dynamic evolution of culture. There was a time, in the 19th century, when artists spoke for their communities and for civil society as well; when their "experimental work" was recognised, as a missionary task, to liberate individuals "from the smug of the middle-class audience, which responded with scorn and outrage" (Bell 1972, p. 15). The manner in which avant-garde artists changed their relationship with the public, until they managed to create their own audiences, inspired social reflection on the relationship between governors and governed people, between majorities and minorities, between notorious figures and marginal individuals. Whenever the arts set the taste for the public, as well as the trends for the cultural market, societies embrace a new stage of liberation.

On the other hand, modern societies embody dominant forms of culture, as "products of public deference to museums, commercial galleries and the news media" (Ackerman 1969, p. 378) and unconventional, or adversary forms of culture. They represent, according to Bell, the victory of the revolutionary, of the new culture itself, not the victory of an expert, or a professional. Culture is detached, meaning "self-determining" (Bell 1972, p. 17). Progressively, dominant forms of culture feel they are under attack and begin to behave as "adversary cultures," and the new forms of culture, which debuted as adversary, meaning reactionary and transgressive as opposed to classical structures, are more and more enunciated as the fundamental. Cultures are subversive, if we accept Lionel Trilling's argument: they impose habits of thought. What performs as an adversary culture will soon become a dominant one. This logic, through which any revolutionary form of culture becomes an epigone at a certain point, so that any transgressive movement gets to be a classical one once it is adopted, widespread and gains dominance, highlights that at a social level, the orchestrators of these paradigms influence society and not vice versa. Society is the ultimate product of these rebels, "hierophants of culture" – "painters, writers, film-makers" (Bell 1972, pp. 17–18).

2.3 Radical Cultures, Cultures of Radicalism. "The Aberrant Decade"

Conventionally, modernity is distinguished as a historical relationship between a historical ethos that begins with the *Cartesian moment*, in the 15th century when the Renaissance and the Reformation revealed modernity as the clash between the cultural revolution of the bourgeoisie and the spiritual revolution of the middle and lower classes, and an artistic moment of explosion, when the tradition of the new invaded the year 1850. In *The Painter of the Modern Life*, Baudelaire explains that the middle of the 19th century imposed the reorientation of modernity towards the ephemera, the fugitive, the transitory and the contingent, as categories of our modern sensibility. As this weak and postromantic thought invaded the milieus of cultural creation, the Marxist critique of capitalism became widespread throughout Europe. At the beginning of the 20th century, the two world conflagrations and their synchronicity with the culture of the avant-garde prepared the field for a certain culture of radicalism. Drastic changes were required in order to reconfigure modern society, its ideals of freedom, independence and security. At the same time, this reactionary culture of the post-war reflected the need to reflect authentically on a new form of alterity. Who decides for me? Whom can I trust? How can we govern together in order to prove that democracy is achievable and maintainable? The 1950s are, for Daniel Bell, the point of departure for a decade of "conservatorism and cultural bewilderment" (Bell 1972, p. 18).

The "aberrant decade" of the 1950s (Figure 2.1) was followed by "the radicalism endemic" period of the 1960s – in this regard, the French revolution from May 1968 is paradigmatic. Between these two decades, the culture of disillusionment appears: Stalinism is abolished, especially by intellectuals, Poland claims political independence influenced by the changes that the Soviet Union crossed, Hungary isolates Russians and ends their Hungarian Communist orientation. Bell recalls, in this context, the theory of the "end of ideology" to which such historical events contributed. Conceived by Raymond Aron, this sociological theory considers that disillusionment favours the fertile trend of political radicalism, built on the relics of the already classical mentality of shutting down bourgeois values. After the 1950s, radicalism continued, not through politics, but through culture, and this is one of the most important theses launched by Daniel Bell. The inheritance of a half-century of death camps and fear is reflected by the

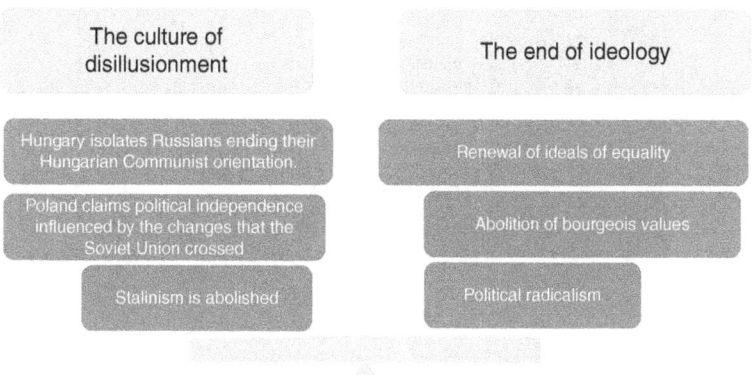

Figure 2.1 The culture of disillusionment and the end of ideology are considered the constitutive elements of the cultural paradigm represented by "the aberrant decade."

Photograph/table conceived by the author.

challenge to rethink the atomisation of society and the values of individualism, freedom and tolerance, after the totalitarian terror. For Bell, this is how culture restores radicalism: Kafka (1971) anticipates bureaucracy, Kierkegaard's embracement of faith (see 1983) instead of rational belief is reconsidered, Weil (1972) proposes her theory that modern societies need new paths to understand grace, Camus "scrutinizes the moral paradoxes of political action" (Bell 1972, p. 20; see also Camus 1955) and Ionesco (1960) reinstalls silence, as a possibility, through absurd.

The 1950s made most of the theory of consumption and mass-society. High consumption alienates individuals and suppresses authenticity. Individuals are inserted into social orders depicted as masses, in which they try an atomistic lifestyle. The quantity of consumption and commodities creates a pretext to interrogate the quality of life. Political life is exhausted – the "cultural *intelligentsia*" represented by "despair, anomie, and alienation" developed the generation of *The Catcher in the Rye*. Culture means organising consumption and

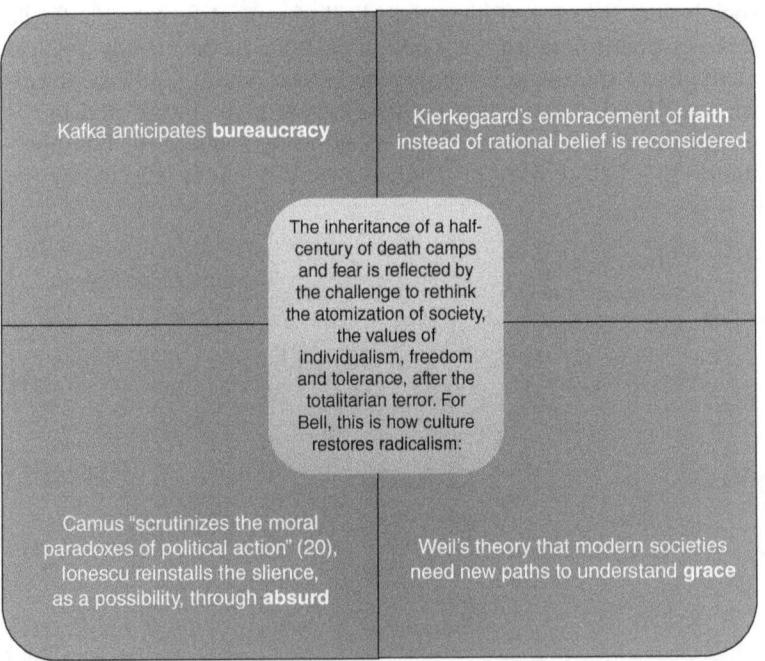

Figure 2.2 Culture restores radicalism by bureaucracy, political action, new models of faith and rational beliefs.

Photograph/table conceived by the author.

consuming organised life. On the one hand, cultural criticism embraces the journalistic formula: mass magazines, in search of popularity, publish essayistic amendments to contemporary lifestyles. The traditional distinctions between high culture and low culture are restored by isolating kitsch from "real art", vulgar creations from real standards of taste. Some of the most important critiques of this decade still insist that society and culture have been in tension since the beginnings of humanity. Bell recalls Arendt's observation that blends classical arguments with historical Marxist premises: the bourgeois – understood as educated people with high standards of life – have always treated culture as a commodity and "had gained snob values from its exchange" (Bell 1972, p. 22). A certain snob attitude was unavoidable and it was, somehow, a trademark for the kitsch of that time. However, if in the first waves of modernity, individualism emerged from such contexts, as an escape from society, nowadays it is a sign of remaining rooted within society. Cultural things have become social commodities.

Here is Daniel Bell, providing an interesting insight on the political impulses of the 1960s:

> In sum, though in the 1950s there was a burning out of the radical political will, this radical will – the distancing of self from the society – was maintained in the culture and through cultural criticism. When new political impulses arose in the 1960s, radicalism found the values of the adversary culture – the attack on society through such themes as alienation – as the Ariadne's thread which allowed it to emerge into a bright, new radical era.
>
> (Bell 1972, p. 23)

2.4 A Sociological Puzzle: Contrastive Cultures and the New Role of Art

The critique of the social structures blended with the cultural need to enforce radicalism as an ideological door towards individualism and authenticity configured what Bell identifies as "a cultural temper", namely modernism: "the self-willed effort of a style and sensibility to remain in the forefront of advancing consciousness" (Bell 1972, p. 23). There are two major social tasks that the 19th century advanced: the urgency to develop a sensitive perception of society as a cultural environment and the need to conceive, in such context, the forms of consciousness that the individual develops depending on multiple cultural agencies.

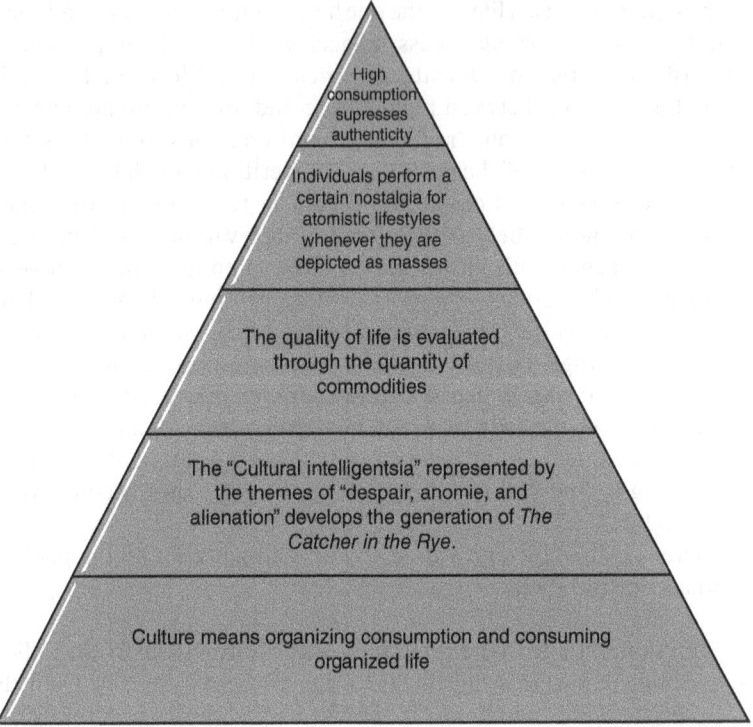

Figure 2.3 Cultural effects of the "aberrant decade" are considered to be the increased public orientation toward consumption and the rise of mass-cultures.

Space and time, the obsession of the first stages of modernity, are substituted by the dependency on speed and sound, that are used to generate revolution in all aspects of our life: communication, entertainment, transport. Consequently, art is no more contemplative and mimetic, but performative and abstract. Moreover, art empowers the spectator and not vice-versa. Aesthetic experience develops a new form of culture that behaves radical by itself: experimentalism is preferred by Impressionism, the concentrated motions and the century of the speed shapes the ideals of Futurism (see Marinetti 2006), the ideals of liberation appear suggested by the dislocation of Cubism, the symptoms of adversary cultures are vigorously reflected by the anti-art forms of Dadaism (see Tzara 1981), the consumption culture is criticised through the shock of the ready-mades. In the end, Bell was right arguing that all these principles, values and shifts allowed "the aesthetic disaster itself to become an aesthetic" (1972, p. 26). Spirituality collapses and needs

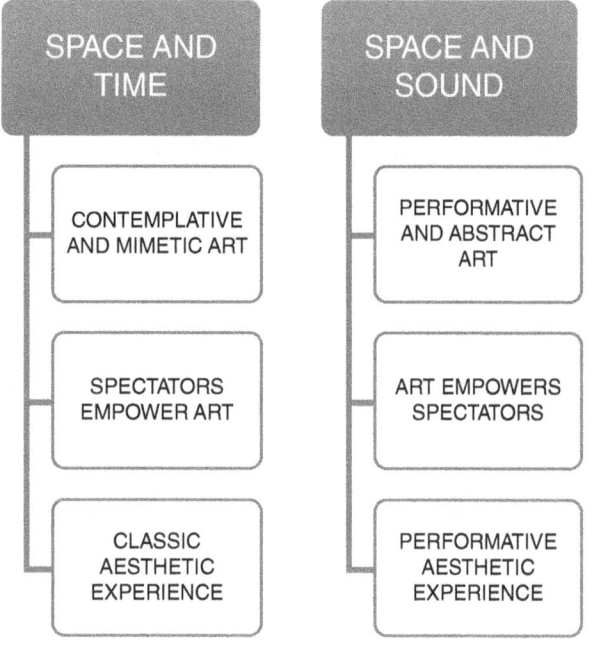

Figure 2.4 Contrastive cultures are determined by two relationships: one reflecting the role of space and time in educating mentalities, and one depicting the criteria of speed and sound in measuring the operativity of different cultural models.

new interrogations, and Faust is there to test the traces of God in man and the echoes of the modern faith in the "godlike knowledge".

Metaphysical grounds are invoked to discuss the possibilities that modern individuals have to adapt to these radical changes that require, for our history, the conciliation between the ideal of freedom and the Hegelian unhappy consciousness. Modern individuals are transgressors of limits: their curiosity goes far "beyond morality, beyond tragedy, beyond culture". By this attitude, modernism rejects hierarchies, reconfigures the paths towards the conciliation between the passions of the human soul – so disputed by Descartes, Hobbes and Rousseau – and the exigencies of the intellect, reconsiders morality as a set of inherited values that keep individuals away from their sensitive and authentic relationship with liberty.

According to Bell, "Economic meliorism, antislavery sentiment, women's rights, the end of child labour and cruel punishments became the social issues of the day" (Bell 1972, p. 26).

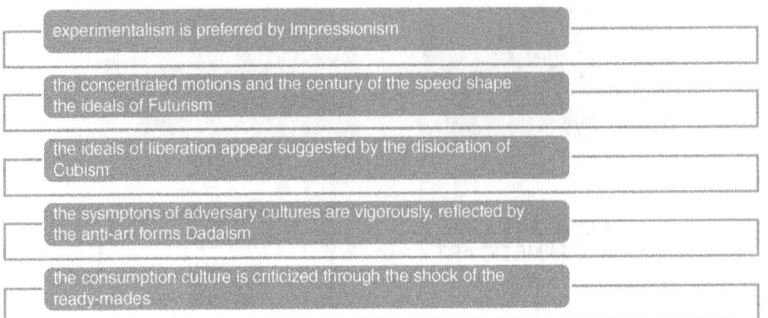

Figure 2.5 Artistic revolutions perform radical changes that will support
political liberation, adversary cultures and consumption patterns
of artistic production and distribution.

But this new society that deals with such problems confronts, none-
theless, a political impasse. What kind of political model fits these
cultural revisionary attitudes? As far as we can see, modern culture
impregnates society with a sense of ending: decadence is a cultural
apocalypse. Discussing modernism, Bell argues that political categories of the spectre, "left and right make little sense". Thomas Mann
was right, considering modernity a powerful advocator of "the sympa-
thy for the abyss". If Nietzsche was a rightist and the French revolu-
tionaries from the 1968s were leftists, does it make any difference for
what their radicalism really meant?

In fact, Daniel Bell was right: "But whatever the political stripe, the
modern movement has been united by rage against the social order as
the first cause, and a belief in the apocalypse as the final cause" (Bell
1972, p. 28).

Affirming life meant allowing the individual to be driven by
impulses, creative energies and provisory pleasures. Life has aesthetic
justifications: this argument will germinate the postmodernist mood,
as Bell calls it, that militates for "acting out", for maintaining the subversive attitude of art defying the rationality of form and content,
taking the artistic content down to the street, in the garage of an individual, in a bar, in all the unconventional places for aesthetic and cultural exposure. Culture happens – this is the real moral of an artistic
happening. Spiritually, Gnosticism formulates new explanations that
leave the cultural taboos of our civilisation apart. On the one hand,
the postmodern character of our society follows a negative Hegelianism
as a theoretical model for constructing our reality. To get to be part of
society, the individual has first to deconstruct it. Bell appreciates the

Foucauldian remarks to this historical situation that reveals not the collapse of the Occident, but the decadence of all civilisation. On the other hand, the postmodern mood starts from the crisis of middle-class values: new theories and popular trends appear, as we need a powerful reassessment of liberation, sexuality, consumption, eroticism, civility. Postmodernism is the inheritance of a century of antibourgeois culture. Nowadays, we have an indestructible appetite for the new. It does not matter what the new looks like. This negative culture, in fact, affirms something: the end of nomianism – hence, antinomianism appeared, the end of forced and formal institutionalisations – thus, the anti-institutionalism. The rationality that organised our life taking inspiration from the bourgeois has no longer partisans or defenders in culture, albeit it keeps its cultural respectability.

2.5 Phases of Cultural Revolutions

Contemporary history is transgressed by the disjunction of cultural and social structures. There are two major revolutions that emerge from this clash, as Bell puts it, one that demands to erase the border between art and life, the other one that insists on extending cultural circles to cultural scenes.

Phase 1. The autonomy of culture was achieved in art, and now it becomes more and more impregnated into the arena of life. "Anything permitted in art is permitted in life as well" (Bell 1972, p. 30).

Phase 2. The social structure that was preferred for cultural revolutions, meaning small groups of intellectuals, the French "cenacle", is now extended at a large scale. The minority that animated a cultural trend shifts towards a large-scale audience, because what was restricted to the elites is now popularised and opened for the masses.

The combination of these two changes adds up to the beginning of a major onslaught by the culture against the social structure
(Bell 1972, p. 30)

Implicitly, markets developed where social and cultural structures interact. This is the main reason for which radical changes are not allowed only as changes in sensibility, but also as changes in society. The ethics and the temper of change appear absorbed by this relational category, culture-society. Between these two relative terms, politics develops as an inner struggle concentrating the tensions between tradition and modernity. Counter-cultures impose counter-structures of society. As liberalism affirmed in economy, society became reshaped by the trends of monopole, competition, cartelisation, production. Growth and poverty are the new actors of our society, instead of bourgeois and proletarians.

By this contrast, we can easily observe that capitalism is subjected to a cultural contradiction, which is inherent. The industrial society, such as the consumption society, operate principles that require rationality: efficiency, maximisation, optimisation, as Bell observed. However, capitalist culture insists on "anticognitive and anti-intellectual currents, rooted in a return to instinctual modes" (Bell 1972, p. 29). So, if practical rationality invokes prediction, universal and infallible mechanisms of decision-making, meritocracy, technocracy and bureaucracy, sensitivity prescribes freedom and authenticity as "apocalyptic moods and antirational modes of behaviour" (1972, p. 29). Cultural contradictions overlap to the fall of the West, to the crises of the Occident and to the impasses of modernity as a whole.

Questions: Evaluation

Task

Choose a form of cultural capital and apply Bell's theory, identifying and explaining a cultural contradiction that lies at the core of your example. What is modern and what is antimodern in the natural tendencies of development of that form of cultural capital?

References

Ackerman, James S., 1969, "A Theory of Style," in *Journal of Aesthetics and Art Criticism*, Vol. 20, No. 3, pp. 227–237.

Bell, D., 1972, "The Cultural Contradictions of Capitalism," in *The Journal of Aesthetic Education*, Vol. 6, No. 1/2, pp. 11–38, available at https://doi.org/10.2307/3331409, visited on August 25, 2022.

Bell, D., 1978, *The Cultural Contradictions of Capitalism*, Basic Books, New York.

Camus, A., 1955, *The Myth of Sisyphus and Other Essays*, trans. by J. O'Brien, Vintage Book, New York.

Descartes, R., 2017, *Discourse on the Method*, CreateSpace Independent Publishing Platform, Scotts Valley, CA.

Ionesco, E., 1960, "Rhinoceros", in *Rhinoceros and Other Plays*, trans. by Derek Prouse, Grove Press, New York, pp. 3–108.

Kafka, F., 1971, *The Complete Stories*, ed. by N. N. Glatzer, with a foreword by J. Updike, Schocken Books, New York.

Kierkegaard, S., 1983, *Fear and Trembling/Repetition: Kierkegaard's Writings*, Vol. 6, ed. and trans. by Howard V. Hong & Edna H. Hong, Princeton University Press, Princeton, NJ.

Marinetti, F. T., 2006, "The Futurist Manifesto," in G. Berghaus (ed.), *Critical Writings: New Edition*, trans. by D. Thompson, Farrar, Straus and Giroux, New York, pp. 11–19.

Tzara, T., 1981, "The Dada Manifesto," in Robert Motherwell (ed.), *The Dada Painters and Poets: An Anthology*, The Belknap Press of Harvard University Press, Cambridge, pp. 76–82.

Weil, S., 1972, *Oppression and Liberty*, Ark, London.

3 Eurocentric Attitudes Towards Modernity and Capital(ism)

3.1 The European Roots of Capital and the Protestant Roots of Capitalism

The main challenge is to understand the historical and ontological priority of capital in front of capitalism. Capitalism is considered one of the most important products of modernity, so capital might prove to be a bastard: its origins are not rooted in modernity, but in the first material forms of accumulation that reflect, in the terms of a natural state, a certain possession. Authors such as Weber insist on the modern trajectories of capital and capitalism, given the fact that Protestantism, as reaction to Renaissance, cultivated an ascetical sense of work that encouraged exchange and cooperation among individuals, whereas voices such as Braudel's argue that capital is a transhistorical notion, reduced to the meaning of an accumulation later engaged into a certain form of exchange, the ideological component, symbolized by the addition of "-ism" being indeed a modern construct. The modern or nonmodern (not antimodern) character of capital is important for the purpose of our research only in order to address a modern platform for the rise of cultural capitalism.

3.2 Western and Eastern Paternities of Capitalism

One of the major concerns of the modern history of capitalism is to explain the European economic split between "the West" and "the Rest" other than the inheritance of the classical tension performed by the Occident and the Orient. This challenge is possible if Braudel's thesis that the capital is not a modern invention, but a tangible reality, concretized since the 15th century is accepted, and therefore its primary role in modernising Europe, and implicitly creating the rise of the West as an economic and cultural power, should be reconsidered.

DOI: 10.4324/9781003329855-4

WEBER

1. capitalism is the invention of Protestantism, therefore it has a fundamental modern character

2. capitalism rises in the West, based on the spiritual crises of modern societies animated by the middle and lower classes

BRAUDEL

1. capitalism is a modern ideology, capital is ahistorical.

2. capitalism is economically related, capital is culturally related.

Figure 3.1 Weber and Braudel argue differently the origins of capitalism: the former considers capitalism rooted in Protestantism, whereas the latter supports the thesis that capitalism is modern, and capital is ahistorical.

Photograph/table conceived by the author.

But the main aim of this critical inquiry is to confront a notorious prejudgment that any researcher of the history of capitalism, even in a philosophical key, has to deal, that of assuming capitalism as exclusively the creation of 'the modern world', "-or, if we wish to avoid the pretentious term 'world', which extends rather unduly the sphere of our own existence, the conception of modern civilisation as developed in Europe and America" (Troeltsch 1912, p. 9) claiming, necessarily but not sufficiently, Protestantism at its origin. As a matter of fact, capitalism is rather associated with the shift from a civilisation of ecclesial authority to a one characterised by the faith in progress, stimulated by Protestantism, but popularly adopted by ordinary individuals in a secular perspective on life and its demands, as counterpart. However, these hermeneutic reactions are founded on a symptomatic analysis of capitalism as the sense gained by the modern era in disputing an authoritative source of its native autonomous individualism and conscious creation of a self-disciplined society. The immediate risk of this analysis is, of course, attributing capitalism to an optimistic approach of progress and to an individual and confident creation of the self, detached from the hyperbolical scepticism of a Christian pessimism based on the influences of two dogmatic presuppositions – *punishment* and *redemption* – on organizing the social life.

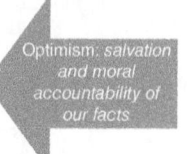

THE CONSTRUCTION OF THE
MODERN SOCIETY
CATHOLICISM VS. PROTESTANTISM

Pessimism: –
punishment and
redemption –

Optimism: salvation
and moral
accountability of
our facts

Figure 3.2 Catholicism and Protestantism engaged different metaphysical perspectives in the rise of modern society.

Photograph/table conceived by the author.

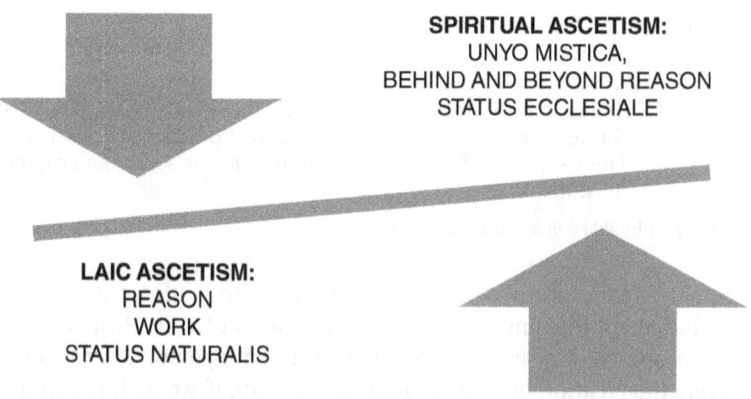

SPIRITUAL ASCETISM:
UNYO MISTICA,
BEHIND AND BEYOND REASON
STATUS ECCLESIALE

LAIC ASCETISM:
REASON
WORK
STATUS NATURALIS

Figure 3.3 Laic and spiritual ascetism invested capitalism with different values and perspectives.

Photograph/table conceived by the author.

Is it worthy to reduce capitalism to the effect of the hostility of these metaphysical alternative models to explain societal structures as well as their welfare, or to argue that without religious individualism, its modern character cannot consistently be justified?

Partisans of the Protestant ethics and its premises for arising capitalism, mainly as a Western proof of individual emancipation, reflected on modelling a modern professional ethics after religious asceticism, advocate for an affirmative answer. Weber, Troeltsch and Tillich opened this argumentative path in favour of presenting the capital as a Protestant cultural product. How fragile are these positions, though, if one would confirm that the capital is not 'a modern invention', nor an originally religious one? According to Troeltsch,

Since Protestantism has a special significance for the development of this religious Individualism and its extension to the whole range of common life, it is clear from the outset that it has had no inconsiderable influence in producing the modern world. And this has always been recognized, whether as a matter for praise or blame, except by those who wish to derive the whole origin of the modern world from the Renaissance, or even from the age of the positive sciences which succeeded it.

(Troeltsch 1912, p. 40)

Therefore, fear of excess of freedom, as it is depicted by modern society, combines values inspired by religion, and becomes a consequence of the metaphysical clash between Protestantism and Catholicism, with multiple effects on the ideological characteristics of capitalism.

What if Protestantism inherited a specific notion of "capital" and performed it in the terms of a new epochal paradigm – that of rational individualism – emancipated from the authority of ecclesial discourses and dogmatic determinations of its further ideology? Then, the entire sense of the modern world could be reinterpreted.

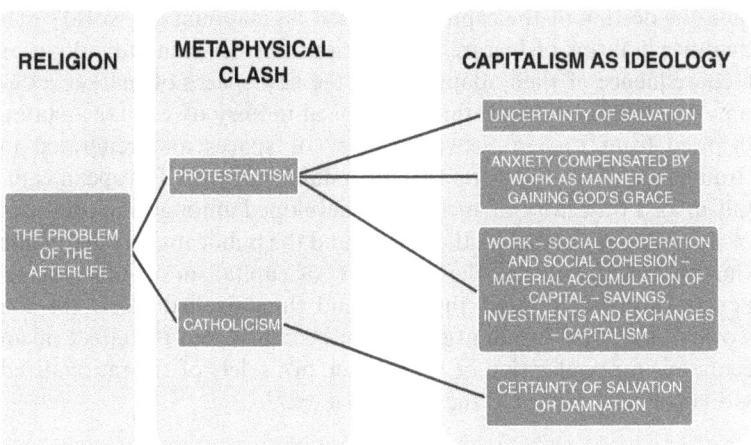

Figure 3.4 Fear or excess of freedom represent two core-attitudes of capitalist lifestyles, determined by religious assumptions and their subsequent metaphysical imbedded paradigms.

Photograph/table conceived by the author.

3.3 Braudel's Theory on the Dynamics of Capitalism and its Modern Traits

According to Braudel, capitalism was not created by the modern state: it was "a given", fulfilled by its direct equivalence with the state in itself, regarded as the structure responsible to ensure proper conditions for accumulation of capital, wealth and security for economic actions in a defined social order: hence, Weber's argument, for example, assuming that capitalism is the creation of Protestantism, mainly of Protestant states such as England, Netherlands and Germany, proves to be false[1]; they were only state actors that "fulfilled" regulatory actions for capitalism. On the one hand, targeting capitalism as a puritan cultural product is the result of an economic coincidence. During the first centuries of the modern era, the emplacement of the centre of mass of the global economy in Western European countries, dominated by Protestantism, was misunderstood as a democratization of the economic dynamics, impelled by the consequences of religious dogmatic contents on normalising the individuals' private life, as well as their (material) interaction. The declared Protestant rivalry toward the Catholic dogma of predestination caused the creation of an individual autonomous sense of preserving and valuing the life that became possible independently of whether or not the ontological argument of God's existence is valid. Weber's error consists in claiming that capitalism had the role expanding the modern world, when, in fact, the destiny of the capital depended on mapping the world's inequalities in terms of hierarchical relationships between individuals as a consequence of their adaptation to the new spaces of market economy. On the other hand, this topological inquiry of capitalist states, inspired from Lucian Febvre's theory of spaces and reiterated in Braudel's analysis, supports the understanding of the European capitalism as a trajectory of mentalities developed among four centuries of ascension registered by the private and the public market that made Europe itself to possess the hegemony of capitalism on other continents. Thus, the split of the West and the so-called "Rest (of the world)", as Vries[2] would argue, might be considered the effect of an economic rationalization of the market, not solely of the rationalized individualism proper to "the Protestant era"[3].

> In economic terms, Europe was different – more specifically to the fact that was the first – and for a long time the only – continent where a mature form of capitalism could be found. Braudel distinguishes three layers of economic life: material life, the (market)

economy and capitalism. The fundamental difference between the West and the rest of the world, the difference to which the former owes its leading position, is capitalism.

(Vries 1998, p. 2)

As a consequence, what made Europe typical for capitalism was not only the territorial expansion and its topological dynamics, but also its privileged position 'to become modern' despite other civilisations. The problem is that limits are neuralgic in diagnosing capitalism: modernity never was easily identifiable, at least in what concerns its intertwining with postmodernity, as the capital never was assigned exclusively to modernity. Braudel's opinion is that even though capitalism is specific to the paradigm in which the individual chairs the idea of capital in the production process, while the capital is a simply "tangible reality" (Braudel 1977, p. 47), this distinction has no temporal boundaries and should break the tradition with the Marxist comfortable definition of capitalism (see Marx & Engels 1990); hence, capitalism is not a restricted phenomenon in the universal history to a specific stage of the economic development.

Adam Smith's liberal critique (1982) assumed the exchange of products, goods and services as a canonical characteristic of capitalism. Marx would have emphasized capitalism as the economic paradigm of production based on social hierarchies and inequalities provoked by the exclusive possession of means of production as private property, in which private entails the bourgeois class and, therefore, have no pretentions of universality. Gradually, the definition of capitalism began to become more sensitive to a normative debate: property as possession is less striking; the practices that justify and limit its use seem indispensable from the ideological rise of capitalism. As a consequence, Baechler assumes that capitalism is "an economy where all factors of production are subjected to a specified property rights", oriented towards dominant economic actions, by "the allocation of scarce resources through markets", directly or mediated, and hence, it is obvious to notice that "capitalism is not simple an economy, but also a civilizational condition" (Baechler & Wallerstein 1997, p. 14). A potential counter-argument comes from Wallerstein, who conceives that "historical capitalism should be analysed in terms of changing institutional mixtures, rather than paradigmatic models".[4] Braudel is the one who fights against this radical interpretation of capitalism as being *paradigmatic* (see Braudel 1993). Patterning capitalism is impossible in the light of Braudel's theory: in short, the historical discussion on capitalism must be opened in the terms of its *spirit*. Capitalism emerges from *le grand histoire* and its circulation as a dialectical nature is the one that gives particularity to the spirit that transgresses the inter-civilisational exchange that characterises it.

> Protestantism was instrumental in dissolving the traditional unity of sacred and secular power: it inspires changes that made the whole tenor of social life more compatible with capitalist principles; and last but not least, it gave a more pronounced civilizational identity to the north-western periphery of Europe and put an end to its quasi-colonial status vis-à-vis the regions of old Latinity.
>
> (Arnason 2001, p. 122)

As a matter of fact, genealogically, capitalism should be considered culturally multi-layered: Protestantism was a necessary phenomenon for the liberalization of the market, but its role was as important as that of any other religious paradigm that accelerated a modernisation of the civil society. For Braudel, religion, still "a force of tradition", rejects the trends of the market, the financial speculations and the usury, even if it succeeded, through the institutional expression of the church, to accommodate to all these exigencies. To make the point, the church "accepted an *aggiornammto*, to use the expression coined after Vatican II, or what used to be called a *modernism*" referring to Thomas d'Aquino as the author of "the first *modernism* destined one day to succeed" (Braudel 1977, p. 65). All the formal resistances of the church to the democratization of economy were maintained until the Reform, retained as the reason for the capitalist ascension of different countries from Northern Europe, as Weber considered. Braudel rejects his argument, based on an economic analysis: the North took the place of the Mediterranean old capitalist centres, the switch being caused by the emplacement of the main resources of the global economy in these regions, privileged for the progress of market economy, the monetary stability, and the so-called management of the social hierarchies. Therefore, all the states, within which Weber considers that European capitalism germinated, are natural areas of displacement of the centre of gravity of the world economy:

> They invented nothing, neither the technique, nor the business conduct. Amsterdam copied Venice; London will copy Amsterdam exactly as New York will copy London.
>
> (Braudel 1977, p. 66)

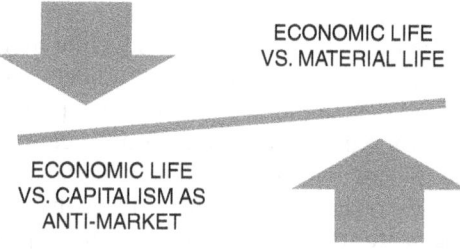

Figure 3.5 Capitalism creates a balance between anti-market perspectives and materially oriented interventions, as expressions of economic life.

Photograph/table conceived by the author.

Following Braudel, one might argue that capitalism is circumstantial. In my opinion, this perspective might serve to reinterpret the role of Protestantism in the rise of the West, depending also on economic conditions, not only on cultural contents, as well as to distinguish different forms of capitalism, mainly classified between an old form, devoted to the constitution of markets and the primacy of good, and a new structure, belonging to the exploration and interaction of capitals. Braudel seems to read the Protestant capitalism in the terms of the first form: it is significant as the age of production and awakens consciousness. In this sense, it is not yet the age of capitalism as destruction, understood in the terms of consumption. Then, what is typically European for capitalism, determining, implicitly, the rise of the West and, moreover, what is capitalism, in the end? Braudel distinguishes *the economic life* from *the material life*, on the one hand, and from capitalism, on the other hand. Capitalism, in its pure form, is an *anti-market*, in which norms of the freedom of the choice are manipulated by interest groups, taking advantage of the lack of transparency of several markets in order to monopolize certain domains of activity.

> Braudel's capitalism thus is characterized by protectionism and exclusion, not by free competition. What Braudel refers to as 'capitalism', would be called 'monopoly capitalism' or 'late capitalism' by Marx and Lenin and 'the industrial system' by Galbraith.
>
> (Vries 1998, p. 6)

In these terms, Braudel's capitalism proves to be a multi-layered construct, both economically and culturally. Firstly, economically, capitalism surprises a dual structure, which combines the material life as a *compositum* of limit-elements for the existence of the market without the constraints of the price or its subjection to a certain mechanism of valuing, with a market layer, in which production and exchange are normalised. In Vries' opinion, continuing Braudel's argument, in the latter, "supply and demand are supposed to set prices" (1998, p. 6). Secondly, capitalism depends on various layers of geographical accommodation and interaction of key-zones, either as representative domains of activity, or as spaces organized through an emergence that begins with the centre of *l'économie-monde* and expands towards a periphery of economic areas. Even though Vries considers this spatial disposition of economic layers being influenced by Wallerstein's theory, I believe that in here, Lafebvre's influence on Braudel, otherwise recognized from the introduction of *Afterthoughts on Material Civilization and Capitalism* is obvious. Thirdly, the history of capitalism, as history of inertias, evolves from a stage of general economic flourishing, that of the 15th century, to a consecution of phases, composed from a period of rising economic superstructures – the 16th century, an interval of recession – known as the 17th century, and a century of economic ascension – the 18th. In this logic, the capitalism is considered immune to the Industrial Revolution: mercantile and industrial capitalism remain similar in what concerns their mechanisms and generally economic norms: technology cannot support, by itself, the entire change of mentality as well as the complex economic consequences of industrialization. It ensures, without doubt, new concerns of the economic life, but industrialization generally refers to goods and their primary materials, rather than to their attached economic patterns of valuing and circulation. Fourthly, capitalism raised in Europe stimulated by laws of inheritance for "family-business": state protection and privileges for capitalists fixed the properties and actions of different entrepreneurs, stimulating the European internal dynamics of capitalism.

According to Braudel this implies that European society experienced less social mobility than important civilisations outside Europe. The view that capitalism is both the cause and the result of permanent innovation attended with social mobility, in his opinion, is only ideology. As so often in history, this, too, is a question of context and nuance. Although Braudel emphasizes the possibilities to establish entrepreneurial dynasties in the West, he is also the historian who, for example, in *La Méditerranée* examines in detail the so-called 'treason of the bourgeoisie'.

(Vries 1998, p. 8)

All these conditions made the West possible. On the one hand, Europe focused on internal dynamics of properties, exchanges, goods, material standards of life, everything that, in a common perspective, might anticipate, as primary elements, capitalism, in a general acceptation. On the other hand, Braudel assumes that for the Occident, capitalism and urbanization are rather similar, if not equivalent. The simple emplacement of the great metropolises or developed cities in the West favoured an autonomous mutual economic interaction, also conceived as force relationships, on which capitalism stands.

> Even more than with the Western state, Braudel connects capitalism, or rather its origins, with the Western city. In his opinion, the city is the perfect place for innovation and as such almost synonymous with capitalism. It is not so much the size of cities he alludes to (large metropolises can be found outside Europe too, and even larger ones), but the fact that in the West cities were – or at least had been – independent and formed a hierarchical network of markets. The fact that Western cities had their own, free 'bourgeois' elites, has left permanent marks on Western states.
>
> (Vries 1998, pp. 8–9)

The entire bourgeois tradition has, as precedent, the project of a feudal Europe, disputing different models of sovereign and power that created all the premises for the modernising process. Nevertheless, Europe was not a singular case in the history of capitalism in this regard: a similar position is held by Asia, both offering a structure of autonomous evolution towards capitalism. But, this contrast serves to approach the rivalry between the Orient and the Occident in terms of Alter-Europeanism: entirely totalitarian, Asia became focused on trade actions in order to satisfy the governmental exigencies of a hyper-controlled economy, even though internally, its cities never reflected a hierarchical disposition, while Europe, attentive to China's needs in this direction for example, performed its development in a natural course, arising capitalism not under the paternity of an "European empire",[5] as Braudel noticed, but as a path to *modernise* the process of state formation and, implicitly, its geopolitical map. Both pre-industrial and industrial Europe are the creation of the European society based on business dynasties and a monopoly of power, also generated in capitalist terms. Profit and power coexist and therefore, they dictate the entire cyclical dynamics of economy.

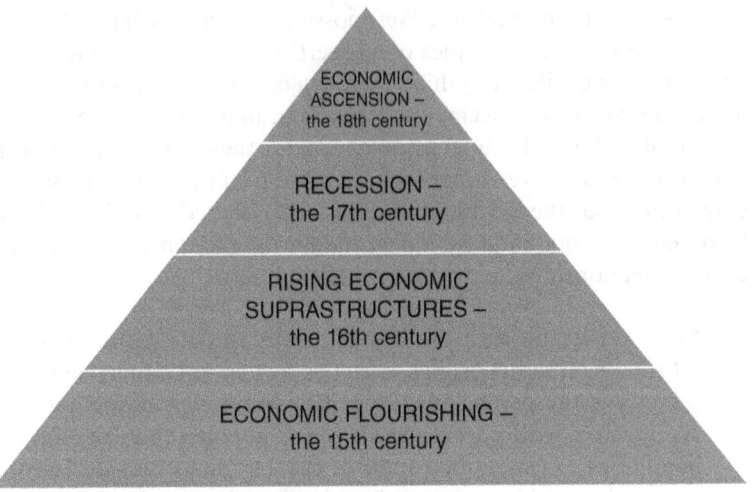

Figure 3.6 Economic flourishing from the 15th century until the 18th century records different capitalist dynamics.

Photograph/table conceived by the author.

These two strategic criteria, fixed by industrialization, are significant for the attempt to understand the reasons for which the West became atypical, or, at least, impossible to be reached by the Rest. Braudel would argue that in each of these stages, the West reflected tolerance for the idea of maritime expansion: from this point of view, Europe's mobility and predisposition to exchange, trade and profit are demonstrated, while Asia remains in the position of the preferential "guest". With a triple population in the early modern era than Europe, Asia had all the chances to attract the Europeans and to host a potential alter-Europeanism between its borders, created through commerce: Asia was receiving the highest quantities of precious metals exported from America to Europe, and, as a consequence, the demographic criterion, as well as the economic value of imported goods recommended it as the ideal platform of capitalist development. Apparently, the non-West had all the premises to be more "capitalist" than Braudel suggested, but what made capitalism authentic was the influence of political structures and organic power on structuring economy and thus, the European political economy can be assumed as a capitalist one, with no restraints.

3.4 Applying Braudel's Theory on Cultural Capital

Braudel's work is incredibly important for historians who seek to connect civilisation and capitalism as one of the most important trajectories of mankind. His methods and style of research, loyal to the School of Annales (well-represented by Bloch and Febvre) have been supported by a personal curiosity on the world history which he seeks to comprehend in order to procure a sense and a structure for the so-called global history.

Macfarlane observed that the metaphors used by Braudel to suggest the time of the history, the becoming of different topological and chronological structures, as well as the ethos of modernity for the Mediterranean civilisation, which he appreciated most, follows the next stages of time division:

Culture is trackable in terms of structures, so large units of time allow its genealogy. In these generous intervals, revolutions occur, meaning changes that involve economic or social concerns, which need decades or centuries to fulfil. This is the example of the industrial revolution. *Evenimential* history is reducible to specific circumstances of high impact, which can be recognized individually along history: battles, revolts, diplomatic agreements. Metaphors emerge from this historical mechanism. History is a big ocean that has unmoving water and waves at its surface. This first metaphor is natural. It is followed by

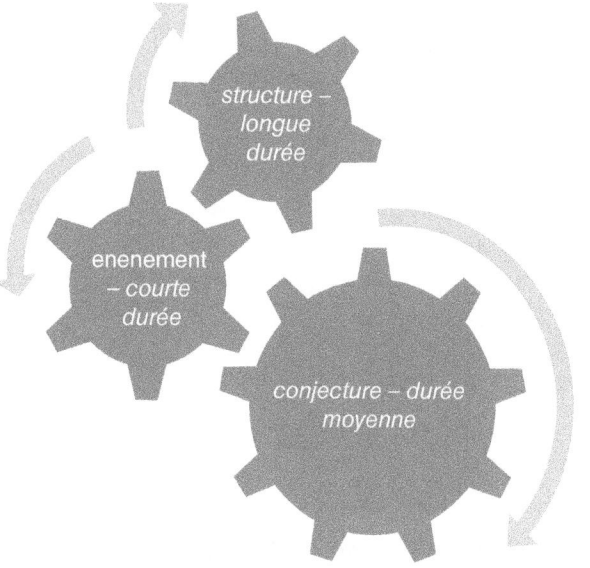

Figure 3.7 For Braudel, the three elements that contribute to the historical dynamics are structures, events and conjectures.

Photograph/table conceived by the author.

a second one, which Macfarlane recommends as genealogical: nonanimated and animated nature evolves, flora and fauna appears, right after water floods the earth. The last metaphor that fulfils the Braudelian dialectics is architectural: buildings appear, with floors and levels, meaning structures and superstructures. Such a perspective reflects a suitable plan for the Museum of the Mediterranean World, for which Braudel "collected objects over the period 1925–1939 and which he laid out in paper during his incarceration between 1940–1945" (Macfarlane 1996, p. 3).

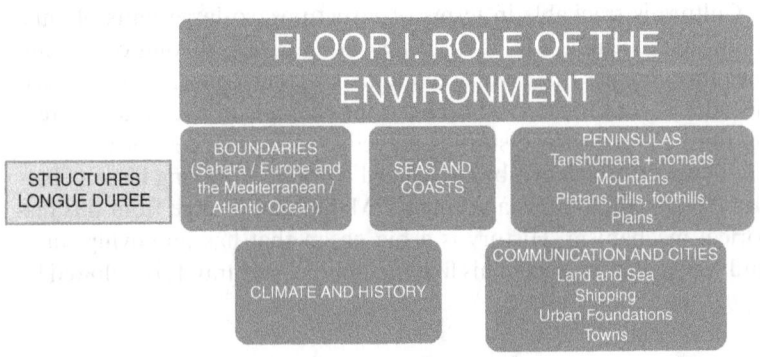

Figure 3.8 The Mediterranean World of Philip II Museum exposed at the first floor the structures or the domains crossed by *longue durée* processes.

Photograph/table conceived by the author.

Figure 3.9 The Mediterranean World of Philip II Museum exposed at the second floor the conjectures or the domains crossed by *durée moyenne* processes. It targeted historical categories such as collective destinies and general trends.

Photograph/table conceived by the author.

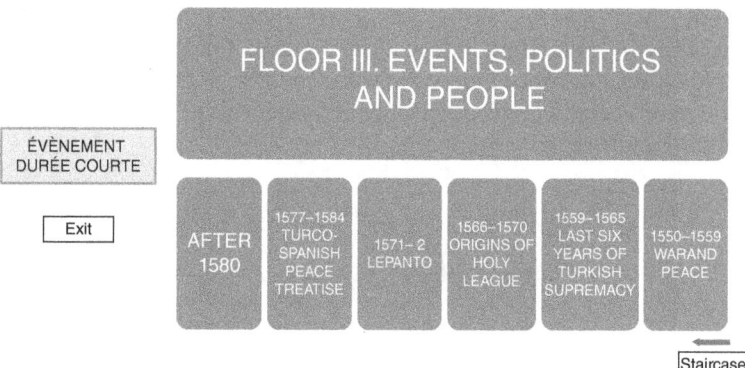

Figure 3.10 The Mediterranean World of Philip II Museum exposed at the third floor the events or the domains crossed by *courte durée* processes. The focus was on three historical categories: events, politics and people.

Photograph/table conceived by the author.

This structure is not quite relevant for a sociologist, nor for a philosopher. For a historian the project of such a museum, as a heterotopy, will be of higher importance as longue as it configures the spirit of the Mediterranean civilisation, in quite a genealogical form. But this sketch has been included here because it reflects the application of Braudel's theoretical model of the evolution of a European civilisation in three stages, a paradigm that led to a second sketch, this time belonging to the *Civilisation and Capitalism* Museum. The base is composed by the material civilisation, followed, at the second floor, by the economic life and, at the third floor, by the superstructure of high capitalism. Macfarlane considers that the first museum is the project of an incarcerated man. Therefore, its structure is almost non-Braudelian. The second museum has been supervised by Bell, and it surprises the Mediterranean civilisation in its stages of higher flourishment and societal boom.

> The first Museum was created in a period of slow growth in historical knowledge and helped to found a new discipline. The second construction occurred while the world of social and economic history was expanding exponentially.
>
> (Macfarlane 1996, p. 7)

Braudel develops the sketch of a *Museum for Civilisation and Capitalism* by generating independent domains for the structures of everyday life, the wheels of commerce and the perspectives of the world. Culture, and more specifically, certain forms of cultural capital emerge from here:

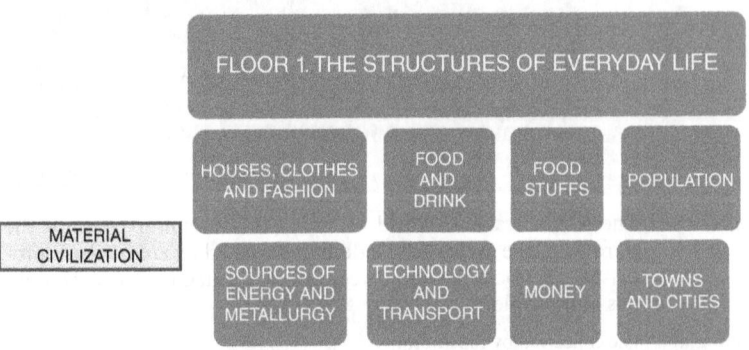

Figure 3.11 The first floor of the Museum of Civilisation and Capitalism provided insights on the structures of everyday life.

Photograph/table conceived by the author.

Figure 3.12 The second floor of the Museum of Civilisation and Capitalism provided insights on the wheels of commerce.

Photograph/table conceived by the author.

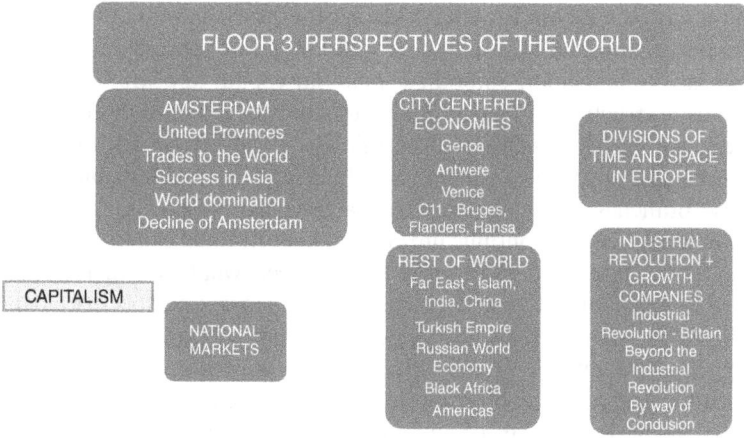

Figure 3.13 The third floor of the Museum of Civilisation and Capitalism attempted to depict perspectives of the world on welfare and progress.

Photograph/table conceived by the author.

Macfarlane observed that Braudel neglects religion, which became a missing area from his imaginary museum of the European capitalist civilisation. Implicitly, the correspondent institutions of the spiritual life are missing – churches, communities from which practices and spiritual beliefs, as immaterial or intangible forms of cultural heritage emerged. One possible explanation might be that power became subtler. However, institutions of power, in a political, not a spiritual sense, are equally missing – administration is represented by taxation structures, but political structures of law are absent. The aesthetic world of art and the axiological dimension of morals are suppressed. Nevertheless, these floors, as they appear in the project of Braudel, are marked by abundance and somehow directed towards his ideal of representing a total social history, by all the means of structuralism. Macfarlane considers that there is little correspondence and articulation between *structure, conjuncture* and *évènement*. The gaps between them are suggested also by his theoretical approach on the relation between state and capital, or between spirituality and culture. For example, Braudel states that capitalism triumph only if it succeeds to identify itself with the state, and that religion, as far as conservative and opposed to capitalism might be, it always passes through a process of accommodation, supporting families as long-term institutions of social growth and wealth. Nevertheless, the most important aspect is to try to deduce from Braudel's sketch of a future museum of capitalism and civilisation how cultural capital might be represented. As we look at the first floor, embodied, material capital appears: lifestyles, domestic structures, practical habits that support the urban and rural life, material instruments that sustain the social dynamics, financial structures that conceive systems of valuing and exchanging objects: all these branches are related to the material civilisation. At a second floor, the so-called economic life depicts what Braudel calls a capitalist mentality. Here, "society, a set of sets" reflects what Bourdieu would have called an objective state of capitalism: theories, perspectives, paradigms, mentalities reflect an epochal manner of exploring the relationship between individuals and capitalism, preparing the field for the institutionalised state of capital. Social hierarchies, state forms of government, boundaries of state markets, and international practices of economy trade represent elements that reflect cultural capital maturing and developing as a civilisational construct. Each form of cultural capital depicted at a national level, for each collective entity, regarded as a state, concentrates revolutionary economic and political practices, certain mentalities of domination, success and decline, and a particular model of alterity represented as inter-states interactions.

Cultural capital is the result of a *longue durée* process. It has an internal logic, subjected both to the *histoire problème* and to the *histoire total*. Braudel will reject a Marxist interpretation of capital as a modern construct (Marx & Engels 1990), and take a more holistic side. Capital is the ground of any material civilisation that rises its structures historically. Capitalism is an ideology that tracks the relation of capital with individuals and objects, in certain social conditions. This is why the West or the Japanese part of Asia became triumphant through capitalism, rather than other parts of the world. Although Braudel's project of a museum of capitalism and civilisation is amendable due to some gaps that belong to a certain historical logic or to some absent segments of the cultural life of a civilisation, his conception is significant as long as it insists on considering cultural capital as an ahistorical construct, that gained its particularities depending on geographical and social conditions representative for each community or nation.

Questions: Evaluation

Task 1

Q How would you modify Braudel's museum of Capitalism and Civilisation in order to make cultural capital more visible?

Task 2

Argue for or against capital as a modern structure, starting from the arguments raised by Max Weber and Fernand Braudel. How do you explain that capitalism emerged from a spiritual crisis (the clash between Catholicism and Protestantism), but later suppressed spiritual values, beliefs and principles, producing the so-called alienation?

Notes

1 I do not share Braudel's perspective that Weber exposed capitalism as an exclusive Protestant product, but regardless such position, his theory on the European rise of capitalism stands as a competitive narrative of framing the genealogy of capitalism as a whole. What I want to stress is Braudel's insensitivity to Weber's authentic remark that the main contribution of Protestantism to define capitalism was developing a proper economic rationalism inspired by its dogmatic contents dedicated to the autonomy of the individual, in the counterpart of the Catholic tradition. It is Weber's opinion that

> on the other hand, it is a fact that the Protestants (especially certain branches of the movement to be fully discussed later) both as ruling classes and as ruled, both as majority and as minority, have shown a special tendency to develop economic rationalism which cannot be observed to the same extent among Catholics either in the one situation or in the other. Thus, the principal explanation of this difference must be sought in the permanent intrinsic character of their religious beliefs, and not only in their temporary historic-political situation.
>
> (Weber 2005, p. 7)

Since Braudel does not exclude Protestantism entirely as determining factor of capitalism, but attests it as a secondary favourable context, in a cultural order, I considered that his theory is suitable for the purposes of my analysis, that is devoted to the examination of cultural distinctions of capitalism in the split between the West and the East, with this prudent amendment.

2 I will use this distinction here, with the amendment that Vries revised his argument, considering that nowadays we assist on the rise of the East in economic terms:

> During the last twenty years of my career I have been studying the rise of the West. That of course is somewhat ironic as these years witnessed its sharp decline and a steep rise of the Rest. We do not need to speculate about a possible decline of the West, here defined as Western Europe plus the so-called Western offshoots: it is an unmistakable fact. The Rest, or at least big part of it, is quickly catching up.
>
> (Vries 2013, pp. 479–480)

For the purposes of the current analysis, his distinction represents the most suitable expression of Braudel's theory on the dynamics of capitalism, interpreted though the tensions between the European model of capitalism and alternative continental patterns, as well as between different internal European structures of capitalist powers.

3 See Tillich (1948).

4 See the critique of Baechler (1995) and Wallerstein's reactions on the clash of theories discussing the genealogy of capitalism, developed by Arnason (2001, pp. 99–125; 2015, pp. 351-357).

5 Vries (1998, p. 9) states:

> The strength of states and cities was often based on the capital available within their borders and on the capitalists' support. In this way, Braudel turns around a quite popular thesis in historiography. Instead of claiming that capitalism could develop in Europe because there was no 'European empire', he claims the opposite: There was no European empire because European capitalism was already strongly in place when the 'empire-builders' appeared on the scene.

References

Arnason, Jonathan P., 2001, "Capitalism in Contexts: Sources, Trajectories and Alternatives," in *Thesis Eleven*, No. 66, Sage Publications, London, pp. 99–125.

Arnason, Johann P., 2015, "Theorizing Capitalism: Classical Foundations and Contemporary Innovations," in *European Journal of Social Theory*, Vol. 18, No. 4, pp. 351–367, available at https://doi.org/10.1177/1368431015589153.

Baechler, J., 1995, *Le capitalisme*, Vols.1–2, Gallimard, Paris.

Baechler, J. & Wallerstein, I., 1997, "L'avenir du capitalisme," in *Comment peut-on etre anti-capitaliste? Revue du M.A.U.S.S.*, Vol. 9, No. 1, pp. 13–35.

Braudel, F., 1977, *Afterthoughts on Material Civilization and Capitalism*, trans. by P. Ranum, The Johns Hopkins University Press, London / Baltimore.

Braudel, F., 1993, *Civilization and Capitalism, 15th–8th Century*, Vols. 1–3, trans. by S. Reynold, University of California Press, New York.

Macfarlane, A., 1996, "Fernand Braudel and Global History," available at http://www.alanmacfarlane.com/TEXTS/BRAUDEL_revised.pdf, visited on August 20, 2020.

Marx, K. & Engel, F., 1990, *Capital. A Critique of Political Economy*, Vol. I, intro. by E. Mandel, trans. by B. Fowkes, Penguin Books, in association with New Left Review, New York.

Smith, A., 1982, *An Inquiry into the Nature and Causes of the Wealth of Nations* (1776), The Glasgow Edition of the Works & Correspondence of Adam Smith, Vols. I–II, New edition, Liberty Fund, Inc., Indianapolis, Indiana.

Tillich, P., 1948, *The Protestant Era*, The University of Chicago Press, Chicago, IL.

Troeltsch, E., 1912, *Protestantism and Progress. A Historical Study of the Relation of Protestantism to the Modern World*, G.P. Putnam's Sons, New York.

Vries, P., 1998, "Europe and the Rest: Braudel on capitalism," available at https://www.researchgate.net/profile/Peer_Vries/publication/282184064_ Europe_and_the_rest_Braudel_on_capitalism/links/560cc48908 ae6c9b0c42d388.pdf, visited on February 4, 2016. (originally published as Vries, P., "Europa en de rest: Braudel over het kapitalisme," in M. Ph. Bossenbroek, M. E. H. N. Mout en, & C. Musterd (eds.), *Met de Franse slag. Opstellen voor H.L. Wesseling*, Leiden, 1998, pp. 238–260).

Vries, P., 2013, *Escaping Poverty: The Origins of Modern Economic Growth*, Vienna University Press, Vienna.

Weber, M., 2005, *The Protestant Ethic and the Spirit of Capitalism*, Routledge, London / New York.

4 The Role of Arts in Supporting the Development of Cultural Capital and Creative Communication

4.1 Is It Possible a Critical Theory on Artistic Capitalism?

Nowadays, considering art under capitalism requires overcoming the traditional attempts of limiting its reception to a concentration of creativity invested with a social function and dominated by market constraints. If the canonical gesture of modern art was "tearing away from materials, ideologies and formalisms" (Bernstein et al. 2011, p. 2), creating an opposite attitude of the early-capitalist art, that of constituting a "symbolic legitimation" (Bourdieu 1993, p. 128) for a class society, for increasing rationality in the cultural industry and for requiring its autonomy as a proper reaction to a politicized discourse, the capitalist art receives the task of facing consumption and its implications for the production of art. The puzzle of capitalist art begins with the need of legitimising art in the social life as a principle of order and self-constitution of the individual, following Oscar Wilde's ideal of regarding our existence as a work of art. How can capitalist art be relevant for the aesthetics of the existence, for inspiring individual liberties and moderated behaviours in the contemporary society of ready-made pleasures, when its own liberty is questioned in terms of art markets, production, reception and popularisation of artworks and institutional practices of exposure? Is art relevant for the quotidian society exclusively due to its function as a "sub-system of the capitalist world system" (Ray 2014, pp. 135–136)? Is capitalist art, after a century of avant-gardes, disputing the liberties of creation, innovation and representational discourses, a new aesthetic revolution, in the middle of the consumption society? Furthermore, to what extent is it possible for it to be both "autonomous" and part of "a social fact" (Adorno 1997, p. 5)? These questions, raised from the challenges that the contemporary individuals face in the assimilation and interpretation of current artworks, reflect the accurate need of developing "a

DOI: 10.4324/9781003329855-5

paradigm of interpreting capitalism through a critical theory" (Boltanski & Chiapello 2005, p. 32). If art is to be considered an independent cultural phenomenon as well as a related social fact, then a social critique should be addressed to artistic capitalism. Upon scrutiny, however, art is inevitably confronted with the paradox of providing the means for an authentic life of the individual in the full era of artificial and technological social experience.

The main aim of this chapter is to examine and define artistic capitalism, by explaining its relevancy and authority as a scientific field of artistic research. I will reinforce Lipovetsky's perspectives on this matter, pointing out the interdisciplinary contents and the correspondent methodology of artistic capitalism. This analysis also questions what kind of social critique is viable for it and what are the conditions that such a structure should respect in order to provide a sufficient and plausible explanation for this cultural paradigm.

4.2 Artistic Capitalism: Norms and Evolutions

For the beginning, I will provide a brief overview on artistic capitalism, which was for the first time enforced as an autonomous domain of research by Gilles Lipovetsky and Jean Serroy in 2013, through their book, *L'esthétisation du monde. Vivre à l'âge du capitalisme artiste*. Here is a core-definition of artistic capitalism, which provides multiple insights on its ideological consistency:

> This is what we mainly call artistic or creative-transaesthetic capitalism, an ideology characterised by the increasing importance of different stages of sensibility and process design, through a systematic work of styling goods and commercial spaces, of generalised integration of art, look and affects of the consumerist universe.
>
> (Lipovetsky & Serroy 2013, p. 12)

Their main argument is that considering the historical power of aesthetics to organize itself around different economic and political conditions, one can easily observe that its main capacity is providing alternative models of self-governing for different societies. In the age of capitalism, its main role was that of liberating the artistic production from the exigencies of industrial culture, inspiring the constitution of an ideal of authenticity for the existence of the modern individual, accommodated with predetermined standards of life and depersonalisation through alienated work. Artistic capitalism engaged the modern era in the challenge of recreating the current society as a work-of-art, following Marcuse's ideal (Marcuse 2007, pp. 123–137). Nevertheless, capitalist society surprises the modern individual in a continuous challenge of subjecting him to the accelerated norms of production and consumption, forcing himself to resist to the routine of hedonist life. Conciliating these two paradigms means, for Lipovetsky and Serroy, finding inside the capitalist society the necessary tools for aestheticizing the world, thus constituting a coherent and consistent ideal of a satisfactory and a moral life. In other words, the production of art and the production of self, understood in the sense of a Foucauldian project of the aesthetics of existence, represent correspondent purposes in artistic capitalism. Life as a work-of-art, as well as art in itself, are discussed in terms of aestheticising the world.

According to Lipovetsky, there are four ages of artistic capitalism, understood as aestheticization of the world. The first one is the age of integrating consumption goods and practices in the quotidian life. Related to this, the two French authors conceive a new definition of artistic capitalism, as "the economic system which functions through the systematic aestheticization of consumption markets, of goods and current environments" (Lipovetsky & Serroy 2013, p. 45). Consumption must seduce the individual and for this, PR strategies, publicity and psychological manipulation of the consumer arise as a social and economic exigency. The second wave of artistic capitalism is that of generalising entrepreneurial dimensions of cultural and creative industries: "artworks get, in this logic, to be judged depending on their commercial and financial results, despite their aesthetic character" (2013, p. 46). Symptomatic for this cultural period is that artistic values are subordinated by economic ones. The third significant period belongs to the flourishing activity of specialised groups in creating artworks or artistic objects, such as fashion brands. Lipovetsky considers, at this level, that economy reveals to be creative in itself – galleries, museums, houses of fashion increase their reputation by their economic power. The last age of artistic capitalism is that of destroying old artistic and cultural hierarchies, as a consequence of what Luc Ferry (1993) would recognise being the democratisation of taste and creation of art. The ascension and overcoming of kitsch, the privilege that contemporary artistic environments bring to technologised instruments of art production, especially in the new media field, the expansion of art to virtual media and immateriality made room, in fact, for a new dynamics of individualisation as self-creation, concentrated on "a decorative market of personalisation" (2013, p. 354) high-life and cosmopolitanism, spectacle and entertainment, hedonism. How could the individual avoid his appetence for spectacle and artificial emotions since the highest-rated artworks are developed, nowadays, by exploiting exactly these dimensions? This question remains open, in order to approach the capitalist particularities of these challenges, in the form of a social critique that I will largely expose in the next section of this article. Up to this point of my research, artistic capitalism reveals being the project of post-industrial era that confronts the autonomy of individual and his self-constitution in an individualist and democratic society, with the double character of art, that of being both autonomous and a social fact. My thesis is that a critical theory should be addressed to the ideology of artistic capitalism, in the traditional sense of Horkheimer's perspective on such a theoretical construction, which aims to "liberate human beings from the circumstances that enslave him" (Horkheimer 1982, p. 244) – in this case, from consumption.

Analysing the manners in which artistic capitalism changed society as a whole, in a historical specificity – namely the industrial and post-industrial era, and reshaping the discourse of modernity by engaging new and particular significances for individualism, autonomy of art, society of consumption, life style and morals, I will argue that such a critical theory is possible, considering some punctual principles, derived from my inquiry. In my opinion, there are two major attempts in this direction: one represented by the Boltanski–Chipello model of constructing a critical theory of capitalism, which applies also to artistic capitalism as subordinated domain, and one extracted from Luc Ferry's analysis on *Homo Aestheticus: The Invention of the Taste in the Democratic Age* (1993). An important mention is that none of them was conceived in the formula of a critical theory of artistic capitalism, but, according to the criteria that I have identified as necessary for such a critical inquiry, which will be later exposed, they can be considered feasible models submitted to this attempt. The main concern of the following section will be the completeness character of each discussed model, observing potential corrections and amendments that could adjust the model of a homogenous critical theory of artistic capitalism.

4.3 The Failure of a Homogenous Critical Theory on Artistic Capitalism: The Boltanski-Chiapello Model and its Corrections

Reflecting on what is called by Gilles Lipovetsky and Jean Serroy as "artistic capitalism" – an autonomous domain of determining art as a social tool for the aestheticization of the world and resistance to all the temptations of a hedonistic life inspired by consumption – involves understanding if this notion explains a new artistic regime, corre-spondent to a historical phase of modernity or postmodernity, or if it represents such a phase in itself. In order to answer this question, I adopted Luc Boltanski's and Eve Chiapello's theory on the four types of capitalism, that I will confront with the four ages of artistic capital-ism, that Lipovetsky and Serroy presented in their book. Hence, Boltanski and Chiapello distinguish between:

(a) capitalism as a source of disenchantment and inauthenticity of objects, persons, emotions, and, more generally, the kind of existence associated with it;

(b) capitalism as a source of oppression, inasmuch as it is opposed to freedom, autonomy and creativity of the human beings who are subjected, under its sway, on the one hand to the domination of the market as an impersonal force fixing prices and designating desirable human beings and products/ser-vices, while rejecting others, and on the other hand to the forms of subordination involved in the condition of wage-la-bour (enterprise discipline, close monitoring by bosses, and supervision by means of regulations and procedures);

(c) capitalism as a source of poverty among workers and of ine-qualities on an unprecedented scale;

(d) capitalism as a source of opportunism and egoism which, by exclusively encouraging private interests, proves destructive of social bonds and collective solidarity, especially of mini-mal solidarity between rich and poor.

(Boltanski & Chiapello 2005, p. 37)

Combining these four types of capitalism in a homogenous criticism still represents a milestone for any theoretical project of reconstruct-ing the main phases of capitalism, according to Boltanski's theory. Each type of capitalism is gathered around some native "indignations" and "nostalgias": for example, the disappearance of authenticity and personal values is confronted with the impersonal domination of the market, while the ideals of equality and transparency are still histori-cally contrasted with the clash of social classes that promoted the bourgeoisie and accelerated capitalism. Hence, Boltanski and Chiapello argue for *a social critique* and *an artistic critique* that should diagnose properly all the insufficiencies of each phase of capitalism. Normatively, the two are constituted independently. My argument is that the first model, that of the social critique, has the privilege of opening a taboo subject for artistic capitalism, meaning "the rejection of any contamination of aesthetics by ethics" (Boltanski & Chiapello 2005, p. 38). Socially, this critique considers that the lifestyle of an individual is modelled by personal aspirations to welfare, reflecting, on the same time, symptoms of decadence and inauthenticity. The artistic mercantilism appears, in the terms of this social critique, responsible for encouraging the reception of an art object as a criterion for social inclusion and validation, since it reflects either the belonging to the same social class, evaluated through the power of making an expensive acquisition, or the homogenisation of the individual's judgments of taste in different masses of consumption, with certain financial standards. The artistic critique will face, consequently, the rational management of the production of artworks that puts in question the social role of the artist, as well as its claims for professionalization. However, during the realist capitalism, meaning the 1950s, this ideal of recognition inspired one of the greatest cultural manifestos, signed by four pop artists that addressed an official letter to the Minister of Education and Cultural Affairs from Westphalia, requiring the social integration of the artist and rehabilitating the status of the art production, as it follows:

Of course today every worker is needed in business or industry but if nothing else should be left for us except to earn a livelihood by working at a lathe or on a construction site after 8 semesters of the art academy it would probably make more sense to take this situation to its logical conclusion and break with tradition, dissolving the painting departments at art schools, including teaching positions and departmental employees. Aged 31 and 27 respectively, we still believe that the visual arts are necessary, also in a time characterized by industry, whether as part of a percent-for-art scheme, as wall-mounted pictures, or as avant-garde experiment.
(Kuttner et al. 2002, p. 32)

Creating policies of recognition for the social status of the artist opened, unfortunately, the Pandora's box of other nostalgias, that for self-creation and discipline. The artist himself became the symbol of the absence of any other artistic production, excepting his self-constitution, depicted as a work-of-art. This shift, from a material creation to a spiritual one, generated the figure of the dandy: in the era of standardized behaviours and consumption, the ideal of aestheticizing your own existence and satisfying personal desires without social constraints appeared as a form of liberty, anticipating as much as possible the hedonist lifestyle that the artistic capitalism proposes nowadays.

However, the two critiques, the social and the artistic one, contain, according to Boltanski and Chiapello, a modernist and an antimodernist tendency. The artistic one reveals itself to be modern when it is focused on liberating the individual from social standards and behaviours engaged to his own subjectivity, and is anti-modern when it proposes the disenchantment of the individual from a social, political or cultural paradigm. The social critique behaves as a modern construct as long as it encourages the destitutions of inequalities, but reacts as an anti-modern discourse in its attempts of criticizing individualism and discussing ideals such as solidarity and social empathy.

4.4 The Social and Artistic Critique of Capitalism

Are these two critiques enough to sustain a larger social criticism dedicated to capitalism and, sequentially, to artistic capitalism? Both Boltanski and Chiapello consider that they fail in providing a unitary apparatus of criticism, since "even in the case of the most radical movements, it (n.a. each critique) shares 'something' with what it seeks to criticize" (Boltanski & Chiapello 2005, p. 40). The lack of a distance between the real and the theoretical realm inflicts the failure of this social criticism, divided in the two models – social and artistic – that are exceeded starting with the 1970s. The authors stress that the former becomes the source for a new theory, demanding the security of the individual, while the latter is reinforced as a theory for the autonomy of the individual. Security and autonomy are not only compatible, but also contradictory. At a first glimpse, they cohabitate in the terms of procuring welfare, comfort, even autonomy. But, in fact, they also synthesize what Daniel Bell recognized as the first age of the cultural contradictions of capitalism (Bell 1979, p. 75), that of accelerating consumption by destroying the old ascetical ideology of savings and abstinence, followed by a second wave of paradoxes, assisted by the confrontation of dictated and standardized behaviours with the morals of authenticity and liberation, concentrated by Lipovetsky's new moral imperative, "Be yourself!"[1]

Hence, what amendments should be addressed to the Boltanski-Chiapello model, in order to develop a sustainable social critique of artistic capitalism? In my opinion, the first problem is represented by the clash between the ethical and the aesthetic level of such a critical theory, which inspires particular "indignations" and "nostalgias" for each of the two aspects of such a theoretical construct, as Boltanski and Chiapello agreed. The key to create the synergy between the ethical and the aesthetic level of interpretation is represented by the attempt to consider them as integrated parts of a modern project of social criticism in which the shift from a Weberian protestant ethic which dominates the capitalist society, to a Lipovetskyan hedonist moral assists the individual also in his quality of art consumer. The social critique should treat, in my opinion, artistic capitalism, in its two aspects – social and artistic – as part of a certain phase of modernity, through which it proves its historical legitimacy, authority and particularity. A similar argument appears in Luc Ferry's pages, who considers that modernism continues, a century later, the work of modern society, that of promoting democracy and liberating the individual from the codes of traditions and mimesis (Ferry 1997, p. 256). In this manner, any model proposed for the social theory of capitalist art should take into account the fact that modernity is focused exclusively on "the subjectivation of truth as primary conception of art expressing a distinct and original individuality" (p. 278). In the line of this arguments, Luc Ferry offers a new solution for the modern tensions between the ethical and aesthetic level of individualism and its receptions in capitalism. His thesis is that there are three significant moments of the accomplished compatibility of ethical and aesthetical concerns on individualism: (1) the understanding of a work-of-art as an extension of the artist; (2) the understanding of science as an objective theoretical discourse guided by the needs of a subject; and (3) the historical constitution of the Subject through the determination of autonomy as value and principle of existence. Hence, excellency, meritocracy and authenticity became the main values that modern individualism operates in the age of artistic capitalism. Even though they are social values, which express human nature, individual aptitudes and efforts or moral criteria for the constitution of the self, they are transposed in the artistic field as marks for the originality, brilliancy and concurrency in the artistic field of production. My conclusion is that at this level, Ferry's model of critical theory of artistic capitalism is successful, since it creates normative correspondences between the ethical and the aesthetic levels of such an inquiry, applying the operating principle of axiological transmutation, which in the Boltanski-Chiapello model was considered impossible to exercise, and therefore invalid.

An important mention is that Ferry's model is adapted, somehow, to previous models of a critical theory of art in the age of capitalism, even though, it was never intended as such an objective. Relevant is, in this concern, the model of critical theory constituted by the Frankfurt School, which is based on two main hypotheses. The first is that art represents an autonomous fact, and the second states that art is a social fact. There are no inadvertences between the two working hypotheses, as Adorno, for example, considered. These two aspects, which inspired the late critique pioneered by Boltanski and Chiapello, in a very popular structure, but with its previous presented reserves on its success, are not accidentally replicated. From the Frankfurt's School, the double character of art – social and artistic – remained a necessary working-hypothesis in any attempt of creating a critical theory of art in the age of capitalism.

4.5   Creative, Revolutionary Communication

My argument is that to the operational principle of axiological transmutation, very efficient in Ferry's model of social critique, some other important hypotheses should be added in order to obtain a complete and homogenous model for such an inquiry. Firstly, bringing modern individualism into discussion involves understanding that the status of the artist has been consequently modified. Buying a signature instead of a work-of-art is the most common example reflected in the jargon of art consumers for understanding the brand-culture as the effect of the exigencies of modern individualism – buying a Van Gogh means an acquisition of $82,500,000,[2] while having a Picasso costs $95,200,000.[3] Secondly, the individuality of the artist represents an authoritative argument for contesting or confirming the aesthetical quality of a work-of-art. The example of Robert Morris' Litanies, "aesthetically withdraw" through a notarial legalised statement[4] signed by the artist is eloquent for understanding the new paradigm for art consumption that capitalism advanced. Art is uncertain; the main quality of an art object being its anxiety: each time, a work-of-art is regarded with suspicion, since it might not be considered to be one by alternative criteria, from other artistic perspective or interpretation. The status of the work-of-art was withdrawn, in Morris' case, through a "verbal exorcism" (Rosenberg 1972, p. 29) performed by its creator. This process opened the de-definition of art, also announced by Rosenberg as de-aestheticization, responsible for creating new boundaries and cannons for the mass production, as well for the artistic exposure. De-definition reflects not only a radical new paradigm of defining a work-of-art, but also the expression of capitalist inequalities, addressed both to the creators and consumers of art. It imposes a simplified production of the art object, mainly through accessible instruments or recycled ones, as the eco-empire of the capitalist aged disposed. On the one hand, this context promoted the expansion of conceptual art; as an example, Morris' statement was considered a piece of art, since it was exposed in different galleries, taking into account the institutional art theories. Rosenberg was asking why a second statement for Morris' withdrawal that could guarantee the lack of aesthetic content for the original document should not be necessary in these terms. On the other hand, artistic capitalism reflects the liberation of art from the dominance of industrial canons, market mechanisms and economic constraints. The echoes of this emancipation are given by the artistic project of Arshile Gorky WPA Federal Art Program, whose objective was to create poor art for poor people. Arta Povera, for them, does not mean low and cheap art, created by inexpensive elements, but the alienated art existent in the art market. At least in the last phases of artistic capitalism, art was engaged in a fervent movement of opposition against consumption criteria for producing and distributing artworks. From the de-definition of art is inspired the third important aspect of a revised model of social theory: art is de-territorialised, based on the fact that the institutional theory of art became old-fashioned and the democratisation of different spaces of artistic exposure begins as a signal of requalifying art as a social phenomenon. The most illustrative example is given by the revolutionary motto from Marinetti's Futurism (see 1909), "Burn the museums!", which anticipates what Dubuffet recognized, in the "Asphyxiating Culture", being the production of a "falsified substitute" for the "free culture", "which acts like an antibiotic" (Dubuffet 1986, p. 8), mostly alimented by the institution of the ministries of culture in different European regions. In a sense, Rosenberg's opinion that the death of art liberates the power of creation from individuals and transfers it to all of us (Rosenberg 1972, pp. 207–208) makes sense only if the contribution of art to the culture and its significances for the society of the capitalist era are clarified. It is true that nowadays culture is understood in two alternative senses, that of "works of the past" (Dubuffet 1986, p. 8) and that of determining the creative intellectual activity, with material or spiritual outcomes. According to Dubuffet, whose radical opinions I do not share but I find relevant for the current argument, State acts as cultural police, creating policies of selection, founding, popularisation and acceptance of different artworks and artists in a national heritage. Regardless the criteria applied in order to realize such a selection, Dubuffet considers that all the policies and public mechanisms initiated by a state are for the social good, which is never the same with the interest of an individual.

To confer a socially meritorious nature to the production of art, making it an honoured social function, is to seriously falsify its meaning, for the production of art is a strictly and strongly individual function, and consequently entirely antagonistic to any social function. It can only be antisocial function, or at least an asocial one...

(Dubuffet 1986, p. 12)

This is why I strongly consider that in order to accept the working hypothesis that art is both autonomous and a social fact, it should be clarified that modern individualism does not interfere with the public life and community. Art for the masses can be consumed individually, or not: as an example, the seductive universe of the 3D and 4D contemporary cinema represents the highest form of consumption culture, addressed exclusively to the individual's expectations, comfort and entertainment. Therefore, individual pleasure maximizes economic profit for cinematic institutions, as well as their capacity to achieve and expose more artworks for its public. But, what Dubuffet targeted in his argument was the expression of free cultural manifestations, assumed as an objective for his *Art Brut* program, despite cultural policies and mechanisms of advertising and public recognition. The artist succeeds in remaining the figure of the individual par excellence when he resists to cultural assimilation: his creative impulses should not be solidary with social expectations on art production, otherwise the entire culture will asphyxiate. What I want to stress here is that autonomy means both liberated creation and cultural resistance in a social field. In these terms, art is still autonomous and a social fact, reinforcing Adorno's perspective: it confirms the former character, by ignoring cultural practices and trends of art production, while the latter character is respected by expressing the art of naïve "outsiders", which are part of the social reality, even though they are ignored or oppressed. At limit, the *Art Brut* program could be treated as a new paradigm of discussing and criticizing the production of art in post-industrial societies, in order to understand the new significances that the double character of art obtained in the last years.

Therefore, in order to understand the contemporary contamination of ethics with aesthetics, artistic capitalism proves to be the most suitable historical interval of postmodernity to be looked at, assuming this task by treating the production of art and the production of human identities in very similar terms. Developing a critical theory of artistic capitalism (see Șerban 2016) enforces the current challenges of reconsidering the social role of art and its autonomy, recently after the century of the dominancy of technical rationality on all the forms of culture and existence, as the members of the Frankfurt School argued (see Șerban 2022). This specific domain of artistic capitalism opens original hermeneutical paths of reconstructing the sense of postmodernity, surprised in the middle of the clash between industrial and post-industrial societies, which provide for the art consumer new senses for the democratisation of the taste, as well as for the consequences of consumption on the lifestyles and authenticity of individuals.

Questions: Evaluation

Task 1

Q Explain how artistic capitalism is considering cultural capital.

Task 2

Q Choose a form of cultural capital inspired by the realm of art and see how the ideology of artistic capitalism and its four phases affects the embodied, objectified and institutional layers of such form of cultural capital.

Task 3

Q Explain the means of creative communication related to the cultural capital prescribed by an avant-garde movement of your own choice.

Notes

1 It is not the place in this article to develop the subject, but a larger argument on this matter is conceived in the first section of the book *Artistic Capitalism. The Consumption of the Work-of-Art in Four Steps: Marcuse, Baudrillard, Debord and Lipovetsky*, in which the author argues that the models of the social criticism dedicated to the artistic capitalism should be theoreticised also taking into account the sum of ruptures that the history of the individualist-democratic society had, as Luc Ferry and Daniel Bell noticed. See Oana Şerban, *Artistic Capitalism. The Consumption of the Work-of-Art in Four Steps: Marcuse, Baudrillard, Debord and Lipovetsky* (Piteşti: Paralela 45, 2016) and Oana Şerban, *After Thomas Kuhn. The Structure of Aesthetic Revolutions in Modernity* (Berlin / Boston: De Gruyter, 2022).

2 The acquisition of Van Gogh's painting, "Portrait of Dr. Gachet", made in 1990, is accompanied by a twisted story:

Up for auction and purchased by Japanese businessman Ryoei Saito, this was – at the time – the most expensive painting in the world. Saito (then 75) caused controversy at the time, stating that when he died, he'd

60   *The Role of Arts in Supporting Development*

have the painting cremated along with him. This was later cleared up as he claimed that he was only using the expression to show his intense affection for it.

M. C. Whinkle, "The 20 Most Expensive Paintings in the World," in *Whudat*, 25 May 2014, available at http://www.whudat.de/top-20-most-expensive-paintings-in-the-world/, visited on July 20, 2016.

3 Picasso's "Dora Maar au Chat" was sold for the second highest price ever fetched at auction, by an anonymous buyer.

Auctioned in 2006, a mysterious Russian bidder took this home (along with a Monet and a Chagall, spending over $100 million) and no one has since found out who he was. The ownership of the painting has still not been made public.

M. C. Whinkle, "The 20 Most Expensive Paintings in the World," in *Whudat*, May 25, 2014, available at http://www.whudat.de/top-20-most-expensive-paintings-in-the-world/, visited on July 20, 2016.

4 His manifesto was signed on November 15, 1963.

References

Adorno, T., 1997, *Aesthetic Theory*, trans. by Robert Hulloot-Kentor, University of Minnesota Press, Minneapolis.

Bell, D., 1979, *Les Contradictions culturelles du capitalisme*, PUF, Paris.

Bernstein, J. M., Goehr, L., Horowitz, G., & Cutrone, C., 2011, "The Relevance of Critical Theory to Art Today," in *The Platypus Review*, Issue 31, January, pp. 2–6.

Boltanski, L. & Chiapello, E., 2005, *The New Spirit of Capitalism*, trans. by Gregory Elliott, Verso, London / New York.

Bourdieu, P., 1993, *The Field of Cultural Production: Essays on Art and Literature*, trans. Randal Johnson, Polity Press, Cambridge.

Dubuffet, J., 1986, *Asphyxiating Culture and Other Writings*, Four Walls Eight Windows, New York.

Ferry, L., 1993, *Homo Aestheticus: The Invention of the Taste in the Democratic Age*, Chicago University Press, Chicago.

Ferry, L., 1997, *Homo Aestheticus: Inventarea gustului în epoca democratică*, Meridiane, Bucureşti.

Horkheimer, M., 1982, *Critical Theory Selected Essays*, Continuum Pub, New York.

Kuttner, M., Lueg, K., Polke, S., & Richter, G., 2002, "Living with Pop – A Demonstration for Capitalist Realism," in R. Storr & G. Richter (eds.), *Gerhard Richter: Forty Years of Painting*, The Museum of Modern Art, Art Publishers INC, New York, p. 42.

Lipovetsky, G. & Serroy, J., 2013, *L'esthétisation du monde. Vivre à l'âge du capitalisme artiste*, Editions Gallimard, Paris.

Marcuse, H., 2007, "Society as a Work of Art," in D. Kellner (ed.), *Art and Liberation*, Collected Papers, Vol. 4, Routledge, London, pp. 123–129.

Ray, G., 2014, "Toward a Critical Art Theory," in Marc James Léger (ed.), *The Idea of the Avant-Garde – And What It Means Today*, Manchester University Press, Manchester, pp. 131–137.

Rosenberg, H., 1972, *The De-Definition of Art*, University of Chicago Press, Chicago / London.

Şerban, O., 2016, *Artistic Capitalism. The Consumption of the Work-of-Art in Four Steps: Marcuse, Baudrillard, Debord and Lipovetsky*, Paralela 45, Piteşti.

Şerban, O., 2022, *After Thomas Kuhn. The Structure of Aesthetic Revolutions in Modernity*, De Gruyter, Berlin / Boston.

Whinkle, M. C., 2014, "The 20 Most Expensive Paintings in the World," in *Whudat*, 25 May, available at http://www.whudat.de/top-20-most-expensive-paintings-in-the-world/, visited on July 20, 2016.

5 Why Is the De-Aestheticisation of Art a Phenomenon Specific to Artistic Capitalism?

5.1 What Is the De-Definition of Art?

When it comes about the idea that the modernisation of aesthetics raised artistic capitalism in the terms of consumption and art production,[1] there are many authors, such as Lipovetsky and Serroy, arguing that this should not be a reason powerful enough to limit the appetite for aesthetics of the current world solely to artistic markets and social behaviours. In fact, a radical philosophical critique of the artistic capitalism started to be claimed as an imperative necessity, since the analysis of the symptoms that converted capitalism, from its native and traditional ideology, assumed by the Marxist theories of production and class differences (see Bell 1979), as well as from the Heideggerian expression of a technical revolution, to an artistic ideology and, more important, to a life style of the (post)modern individual, confronted us with a new social process of claiming the authenticity: "the aestheticisation of the world" (see Lipovetsky & Serroy 2013).

As specific moment of the history of modern subjectivity, this process reiterated Wilde's ideal, the constitution of the self as a work of art inspiring the postmodern project of the aestheticisation of the world, originated, as Lipovetsky argues (2013), exclusively in the artistic capitalism. But this phenomenon appears at the same time with the cultural paradigm of *the de-definition of art*, also named "de-aestheticisation", that Rosenberg understands being the age of "the anxious" aesthetic object: the artistic quality or legitimacy of an object depends on the recognition given by an artist who has the autonomy to proclaim himself as such, as well as to qualify or withdraw his work of art from the function of an aesthetic product. The best example for this argument is represented by Morris's deposition executed before a notary, through which the artist "withdraws from said construction all aesthetic quality and content" of his Litanies and "declares that from

DOI: 10.4324/9781003329855-6

the date hereof said construction has no such quality and content" (Rosenberg 1972, p. 28). At a theoretical, meta-level of interpretation, Rosenberg's project of the de-definition of art, produced in this manner, represents the movement through which the conflict between the traditional art and the art of the avant-gardes became a substitute for a coherent concept of art in our era. At a micro-level, surprising not the acceptances of what art represents generally nowadays, but what its concepts became, one can observe that "the principle common to all classes of de-aestheticised art is that the final product, if any, is of less significance than the procedures that brought the work into being and of which it is the trace" (Rosenberg 1972, p. 29).

The de-definite art is, behind all these flexible assumptions, a correspondent phenomenon for the individual's need to reinforce the constitution-of-the-self through the aestheticisation of the environment, in order to create a minimalist and personalised space for living, or to attach to the consumption the allure of an aesthetic production. If the de-definition of art is specific to capitalism and consumption societies, then it must be understood also as an ideology that encourages the production and the consumption of art. Under these circumstances, Rosenberg revisited his operational definitions for *de-aestheticisation*, assuming that:

> Ultimately, the repudiation of the aesthetic suggests the total elimination of the art object and its replacement by an idea for a work or by the rumour or by the idea that one has been consummated – as in conceptual art.
>
> (Rosenberg 1972, p. 29)

Therefore, the cohabitation of these two apparently incompatible paradigms, the aestheticisation of the world and the de-definition of the art, in the artistic capitalism, requires a revaluation, by applying both a social and an artistic critique.

5.2 Arguments for Raising the De-Aestheticisation of Art as a Capitalist Artistic Phenomena

According to Boltanski, the events of May 1968 must be interpreted in the terms of

> a social critique of a fairly classical Marxists stamp, combined with demands of a very different kind, appealing to creativity, pleasure, the power of imagination, to a liberation affecting every dimension of existence, to the destruction of the consumer society.
>
> (Boltanski & Chiapello 2005, p. XXXV)

This argument might be integrated in a larger discourse, dedicated to the critique of the avant-gardes, as artistic expressions of the will-of-rupture of the individuals, from canonical paradigms of social representation. Therefore, the individual's revolts, in the name of self-determination and unconstrained self-constitution, contrast with his imposture of being part of a large and uniform mass, developing a proper appetence for the art of mass, produced for consumption ambitions. Hence, interrogating if there is any aesthetic revolution in the society of consumption represents legitimate research, once that artistic capitalism promotes both the society of consumption and the individuality of the Subject.

The first hypothesis is inspired by the fact that the de-definition of art represents the result of a sum of ruptures that appeared in the history of 'the individualist-democratic society.' (Lipovetsky & Serroy 2013, 429)

(H1) The de-definition of art is an aesthetic revolution of the artistic modernism, specific to artistic capitalism.

If H1 is a plausible and a sufficient hypothesis, then one should be able to determine what is the protocol or the program of this revolution. In order to give a suitable answer, I consider that in this regard, Luc Ferry's critique of modernism is eloquent: the philosopher argues that the modernism, in a cultural logic, continues, later with a century, the expression of the modern society in democratic order. The artistic modernism liberates the art and the literature from the cult of tradition by exonerating them of the exigencies of the imitation code, in the same manner in which the democratic revolution requires the liberation from the forces of the visible. But, when Ferry sustains "the subjectivization of the truth as main conception on the art as expression of a distinct and original individuality" (Ferry 1993, 223) then a necessary condition should be included in order to accept his assumption: art should adapt also to the individual's will to redefine the ethics in the terms of aesthetics, an aspect that Ferry recognized being a nuclear task of postmodernity. This remark is important because the affinities between ethics and aesthetics exercised in the constitution of the individual's lifestyle, and moreover, in the process of the aestheticisation of the world procures us innovative explanations for the origins and the symptoms of Rosenberg's de-definition of art. There are three significant moments of this relation of causality:

(1) The determination of the work of art as an extension of the artist;
(2) The determination of the science by a dominant objectivity pertained by a Subject;
(3) The historical constitution of the Subject through the recognition of autonomy as value and principle of our existence.

Through these three moments, ethics delimitates three ages of the artistic capitalism, each of them corresponding to one of the next values: excellence, merit and authenticity. My thesis is that the social reception of these values influence, in fact, the production and the consumption of art, the status of the artist and, moreover, his professionalisation and the quality of his works. On the one hand, these values emphasize the role of the artist to apply the notorious imperative of the authenticity, "be yourself" as "will of will" (Ferry 1977, p. 301), to the self-fulfilment and artistic representation of the self-governance practices. On the other hand, the artist renounces a dandy image to express himself both as an individual and as a professional, who devotes the aesthetic object into a perspectival and representational revolution. In my opinion, the fundamental interrogation on this concern regards not the manners in which the artist succeeded in preserve his originality and individuality, but the effects of his existence on redefining the artistic object and provoking, at limit, its *de-aestheticisation*. In the moral hypermodern register, ethicists remark the fact that for the individual, the anxiety substitutes the culpability, while the authenticity is proposed moreover as expression of the personality or as style. Considering these statements, inspired by Luc Ferry, I argue that precisely this revolt of the individual determines the necessity of the aesthetic object to adapt to a series of moral substitutions announcing the artistic capitalism as era of the categorially destitution of the criterions that used to define the quality of a work of art, as well as its recognition. Following Rosenberg's critique, I consider that his aesthetic diagnostics are correct:

> Where an art object is still present, as in painting, it is what I have called an anxious object: it does not know whether it is a masterpiece or junk. It may, as in the case of a college by Schwitters, be literally both.
>
> (Rosenberg 1972, p. 12)

As a conclusion for my arguments, derived from the acceptance of H1, I stress that

(C1)   The de-definition of art, as aesthetic revolution of the artistic modern-
ism, is a direct consequence of the Subject's moral self-representations in
the individualist-democratic societies of consumption.

The autonomy of art, as well as the liberty and legitimacy of the artist
to define or withdraw the aesthetic quality of an object are a natural
consequence of treating the artist as an individual and of strengthen-
ing his professionalisation by accepting his work in terms of independ-
ency, excellence, merit, art market and consumption. Not accidentally,
authenticity became a privileged term despite the concept of authenticity in curatorial discourses, as well as in qualifying different elements belonging to the conceptual art.

This conclusion also inspires a contra-argument to one of
Rosenberg's statements, regarding the changes brought by the individualism to the reception of the artist in the field of aesthetics. Rosenberg
pleads for accepting the fact that

> The de-definition of art necessarily results in the dissolution of
> the figure of the artist (...). In the end everyone becomes an
> artist.
>
> (Rosenberg 1972, p. 13)

I consider that this aspect must be understood exactly contrary,
because it should be interpreted in the light of the postmodern dictum
"be yourself!" The capacity of self-determination and the individualist
revolution for the autonomy leaded to the reception of the artist's figure as individual. This is the main reason for which consumers rather
prefer to buy a signature instead of a work of art, an attitude specific
to the artistic capitalism, as Lipovetsky argued. As a matter of fact, I
consider that the origins of Rosenberg's artistic de-definition should
be placed not only in the radical critique of the quality of the aesthetic
object, but also in the new paradigm of the artist as a professionalised
individual. This is a hermeneutic approach that is missing, as far as I
researched the multiple interpretations that Rosenberg's theory
received both in the philosophical field and in art criticism.
Nevertheless, the absence of such an interpretation is barely caused by
the theoretical critique that Rosenberg himself predetermined, stress-
ing that the de-definition of art as de-aestheticisation is an aesthetic
process that mainly concerns the object of art. *The Litanies* aesthetically retracted by Robert Morris through his notarial statement from
November 15, 1963, a manifesto for the autonomy to deny to any
object created through artistic procedures the artistic condition,

convinces Rosenberg that the artist's capacity of artistic determination is turning aesthetics back to a literalist or conceptual art. The working hypothesis is that the gesture of aesthetic retracting is the act of born of an anxious aesthetic object, anticipating the exigencies of the minimalist Donal Judd, who proposed the emancipation (see Roger 1995) of an art that possesses "the specificity and power of actual materials, actual colours and actual space" (Rosenberg 1972, p. 29). Therefore, Rosenberg analyses two manifestations of *de-aestheticisation*, represented by the aesthetic withdrawal signed by Morris and by the appeal to the materiality conceived by Judd: both argue for the artificialization of the artistic creation. The most important effect of these two moments is the assimilation of the aesthetic withdrawal as *an art of the process*: the recourse to materiality involves the possibility of the destruction of the object, as well as its perishability. The chance of the object to represent a work of art consists of exploring the repudiation of the canonical artistic practices and aesthetic protocols, in order to privilege the function of the idea of a work of art and the rumour of consuming one, which is a perspective with specific affinities for the conceptual art.

H2. The de-aestheticisation of art is reinforcing the concept of materiality of the work of art because it reshapes the theories about mass art production, consumption and exposure.

This hypothesis opens a very sensitive criterion of aesthetic judgment. On the one hand, the materiality of the work of art confronts the nomothetic power of creating an artistic object or performing an artistic act. Morris's withdrawal is not only a precedent in the history of the oral destitution of the artistic quality of an object, but also a legitimation of different criterions of aesthetic proclamation. Rosenberg reminds Morris' gesture as "a verbal exorcism" (Rosenberg 1972, p. 29) preparing the field of conceptual art. In fact, it expresses the very possibility of the "anxious object" to exist independently of its materiality and moreover, to affect the so-called consumption of a work of art in the terms of non-materiality. Therefore, one might ask how is possible for the "de-aestheticized" art to organise the mass production of artistic objects and to influence their exposure? A brief answer is given by the requalification of the artistic experience in itself: either the consumption of the work of art is a *hic et nunc* experience, conditioned by the lack of perennial materiality of the artistic object, or it becomes a multiplied experience whose main characteristic is that of being distributed. Consequently, a second veritable interrogation arises: what senses should claim the authenticity of art in a culture of serial artistic production? It is a sensitive concern for the artistic capitalism the interdependence between the materiality and the authenticity of the work of art: when it comes about a proper materiality, which develops a serial production under the exigencies of capitalism, the authenticity of art moves its accents from the experience of production to the experience of consumption. According to Benjamin, modern technological reproduction adapted, at the beginning, to the bourgeois ideologies of art consumption, *de-aestheticisiation* appearing as denial of canonical aesthetic authority of cultural institutions and artistic practices of production, as well as emancipation of artistic production in the name of autonomy, by destroying the quality of the unicity and singularity, originated in religious traditions that gave cults to the art, and reinforcing it, in very different terms. From production to reproduction, art lost its ritualist performance: it no longer possesses an aura, nor it remains symptomatic for a cultic society.

> The authenticity of a thing is the essence of all that is transmissible from its beginning, ranging from its substantive duration to its testimony to the history which it has experienced.
>
> (Benjamin 1968, p. 221)

Hence, Rosenberg's anxious object inherits only the anguish as expression of an emotional human tangency; in rest, it lacks human intervention for the most part of its creation. Production is no longer natural, it has no "aura" of ritually investment with human dignity: statues, for example, are integrated in society not as cultic artefacts, but as material symbols of ideological control, reflection and personality. In the late capitalism, Warhol's *Campbell's Soup Cans* disputes its pop authority based on the capacity to express the ideology of consumption as base for society manners and lifestyles through semi-mechanized screen-printing processes and industrial practices. As Bourdon asked (1995), if Caravaggio could paint baskets of fruits and Cezanne's impressionism often brought apples into his canvas, why would Warhol's *Campbell's Soup Cans* not be objects with an aesthetic potential, according to the artistic canons of his time? Dominated by minimalism and a revaluation of fine art criterions, his work creates a notorious manifestation of Pop Art in the terms of *de-aestheticisation* understood in two primary directions: the accommodation of an improper materiality of an artistic object to the canons of aesthetic criterions of judgment, respectively the rise of conceptual art in the age of capitalist realism, by inversing the supremacy of the aesthetic experience of production, from the

Pre-World artistic age, with the experience of consumption. On the other hand, mechanical practices of production develop an impersonal art. Rosenberg would argue that this conjuncture favours the apparition of artistic training in the age of artistic capitalism: technology rather prefers practitioners, not artists. In the end, the artist has what I understand as an 'environmental function': he creates the décor, the ideology of context, the subject of the work of art, leaving the mechanical means of production to selectively affect the work itself. In these capitalist terms, the equation *production–distribution–consumption*, applied to the work of art, must be completely adjusted. Hence, the classical spaces of art exposure are reformed, reinforcing the concept of "materiality", but from the perspective of other alternative effects. From Marinetti's dictate, "Burn the museums!" (see Marinetti 1909), art begin to seduce the public space of our quotidian life: mall galleries or street art exposures create the barrier between art and event, leaving the possibility for anyone to be either a performer or a spectator. Art begin to resemble with a public demonstration. Its character of *mass spectacle* created a new artistic paradigm, that of the *anti-art* phenomena. In this concern, Rosenberg quotes Ragon, who considers that the Revolution of May 1968 intimately revaluated the sense of art. Public lamentations from that time were directed not against the market of consumption, the criticist opportunism, the professionalisation of artists, the commercialisation of works of art as a cultural abuse, but against art itself. According to Rosenberg, this mercantile tradition raised by the artistic capitalism tends to treat the works of art as objects, alienated from their subjective experiences of production. From a pre-capitalist age in which both creators and consumers of art lament over the fact that "the artist is an anachronism, his methods are pre-industrial and his equipment is out-of-date" (Rosenberg 1972, p. 205), we get in a fulfilled industrialized artistic era, assumed as posterity of capitalist realism, in which the death of art, confronted with the phenomena of anti-art, "sets free the power of creation from individuals and passes it on to all" (1972, p. 208). In a word, art is deinstitutionalized and this specific cultural revolution is ought to the artist, by breaking the tradition with conformity, in the name of the aesthetic demystification. In fact, this is the century of the remains left by the "portable museum" of Duchamp's *Boîte-en-valise*, a mass production at a very modest scale.

The *Boîte* exemplifies the transition between two worlds: the old Europe of the museum and the connoisseur, and the young America of the commercial gallery and artistic commodity.

(Hopkins 2000, p. 37)

A conclusion derived from the acceptance of H2 is:

(C2) The materiality of the work of arts provokes, in the terms of *de-aestheticisation*, the aesthetic *de-territorialisation*, remarked not only at the level of the artistic production, but also on that of artistic exposure and consumption.

The simple existence of various and autonomous market arts, with very specific trade practices and auction traditions, exhibitions on the lobby halls of corporate centres or informal museums and private galleries, attest the phenomena of aesthetic *de-territorialisation* not only as symptomatic for de-aestheticized art and implicitly, for artistic capitalism, but also as a unifying process of different artistic traditions and practices, independently of their elitist spaces of exposure, in the terms of the so-called *mass-art*. Strictly connected to this topic, a third and last hypothesis of the main argument of the current paper is concretized as it follows:

H3. In the terms of de-aestheticized art, mass culture is the expression of capitalist inequalities, reflected in the aesthetic decadence and indifference.

In order to sustain this hypothesis, I will reinforce the last two of the fourth operational definitions of capitalism from Luc Boltanski's and Eve Chiapello's theory on the new spirit of capitalism and its criticism. According to them,

There are essentially of fours sorts:

(a) Capitalism as a source of disenchantment and inauthenticity of objects, persons, emotions and, more generally, the kind of existence associated with it;

(b) Capitalism as a source of oppression, inasmuch as it is opposed to the freedom, autonomy and creativity of the human beings who are subject, under its sway, on the one hand to the domination of the market as an impersonal force fixing prices and designating desirable human beings and products/services, while rejecting others, and on the other hand on the forms of subordination involved in the condition of wage-labour (enterprise discipline, close monitoring by bosses, and supervision by means of regulations and procedures);

(c) Capitalism as a source of poverty among workers and of inequalities on an unprecedented scale;

(d) Capitalism as a source of opportunities and egoism which, by exclusively encouraging private interests, proves destructive social bonds and collective solidarity, especially in minimal solidarity between rich and poor.

(Boltanski & Chiapello 2005, p. 37)

I have already applied the first two definitions on artistic capitalism from the perspective of the relationship between materiality and authenticity, as well as in the register of investigating the consequences of the autonomous and capitalist process of production of the work of art on its consumption. I consider that the latter significances of capitalism can be suitably addressed to the *Arte Povera* as a specific aesthetic paradigm of artistic capitalism, mainly to the capitalist realism. It becomes obvious the task fulfilled by the artistic discourse to carry on, in representing a social critique, the expression of inequalities both in artistic hierarchies and consumers classes. At limit, *Arte Povera* is a poor art for poor people, as Gorky ideologically explained it. Remarked through an assemblage of poor and artisanal materials, mainly unprocessed, *Arte Povera* belongs to the Italian pre-industrial culture, rejecting minimalism and Pop Art, by a profound lack of synchronisation with their exigencies of technical modernisation of the artistic representation. The humanism propagated by Celant's theorized *Arte Povera* lies on the opposition to the commercialisation of art, enhancing Cage's appeal to perform art as *an experimental condition in which one experiments living*, even though many of its principles align with capitalist views, such as the rejection of elitist or canonical exhibitions spaces, transformed in quotidian dimensions of the immediate landscapes, or the description of primary materials for the work of art in industrial terms, in order to demonstrate "the noblest quality of each one, the most refined technology ... polished marble, cleaned bronze, molten glass, silk worked with dressmaker's finesse and colours to match this context." (Luciano Fabro 1968)[2]

The anxiety of the artistic object seems to be reiterated in the feeling of alienation from nature in the age of a mechanized and industrialized society; for instance, Piero Gilardi confesses, in 1966, that "my attitude at the time was one of anxiety toward the loss of nature, however, at the same time, however, I trusted technology, which I represented in my use of an artificial material: polyurethane" (Flood & Morris 2001, p. 8).

As a matter of fact, *Arte Povera* is not an aesthetic paradigm inspired by penury and economic insufficiencies confronted by Italy in the Post-War period, but a reaction to the American current of democratizing art by commercialising it: the main alienation required by *Arte Povera* is that of the art market, which nowadays represents one of the most surprising utopias in the age of artistic capitalism. The only penury reported by this artistic paradigm is that of the details of art production, returned to the artist in a "natural" way, composed by unprocessed elements, at the beginning, and based on the primacy of the human intervention. It is not a restricted interference to artistic practices of production; on the contrary, it has to inspire a social critique of consumerist lifestyle and cultural institutionalisation of art.

> If life, society and its actual institutions are not open to the freedom of art, then we need to change them.
>
> (Piero Gilardi)

One might argue that the Italian economic recession caused the primary impulse of artists to reinforce natural elements and materials to their work. Their art was the expression of the economic adaptability in creation to material constraints. Therefore, it is not a form of artistic liberty, but the result of a rational cost of investment in art, lately inspiring the rejections of capitalism, considered the main source of this inevitable collapse. And yet, this movement, with no specific manifesto or program, succeeded in endeavouring the return to natural life, testing its possibilities in terms of commodity and comfort, as Mario Merz's work (*Giap's Igloo – If the Enemy Masses his Forces he Loses Ground, If he Scatters he Loses Strength*, 1968[2]) attempts, or in the terms of the inseparability between the artist and its work.[3] Therefore, the last conclusion of my argument, derived from the evaluation of the third proposed work-hypothesis, is:

(C3) De-aestheticized art is also the expression of social and economic capitalist inequalities between individuals reflected in artistic discourses and representations, as well as its consequences on the process of the institutionalisation of art and culture.

This critical inquiry had the role to make the correspondences between Lipovetsky's artistic capitalism and Rosenberg's de-aestheticised art clear and justified, considering that even though Lipovetsky develops a critique of this aesthetic phenomena in his research, he does not refer properly to Rosenberg and his main perspectives on the subject. Hence, the fundamental interrogation of this analysis, *"Why is the de-aestheticisation of art a phenomena specific to artistic capitalism?"* satisfied by the constructed answers previously discusses, paved the way to a new incursion, only announced in here: *"What is the future of de-aestheticized art in the era of artistic (post)capitalism?"* testing, in the same time, the heritage of this ideology.

Questions: Evaluation

Task 1

Q Apply the theory of de-aestheticisation on any form of modern art that you would like and comment the means of creative communication associated with it (manifestos, performances, artistic events).

Notes

1 This chapter is based on my article (Şerban 2016b, pp. 87–102). In order to satisfy a methodological constraint of the current research, I will briefly define the sense in which I operate the "artistic capitalism", enough to clarify to what extent the de-aestheticization is a specific phenomenon for this cultural ideology. I agree, on this level, with Lipovetsky and Serroy's argument that "this is what we mainly call artistic or creative-transaesthetic capitalism", an ideology characterised by the increasing importance of different stages of sensibility and process design, through a systematic work of styling goods and commercial spaces, of generalised integration of art, look and affects of the consumerist universe" (2013, p. 12) because it is not the place for an analysis of artistic capitalism as ideology, I will only mention in here that based on Lipovetsky's perspective, I tried to demonstrate it as the artistic ideology that made possible the aestheticization of the world by unifying the representations of space, time and individual, in a critical theory, which has an artistic component and a social one. This thesis, as well as its main arguments, are developed in a different work, from which the current research is inspired, being an attempt to revisit and finalise the work-hypothesis that constituted, there, the debate on the de-aestheticized art, configured in the first chapter. Şerban (2016a).

2 Curatorial text, available at: https://www.tate.org.uk/documents/234/ artepoveracards.pdf, visited on July 20, 2021. The title of this work, which is spelt out in neon letters around the surface of the igloo, is a quotation from the North Vietnamese general Giap, who defeated the French in 1954. Using earth, Merz refers to nomadic peoples and their shelters, and connects the natural world with our daily lives. The igloo shape was used by Merz repeatedly, usually in conjunction with the Fibonacci series of numbers,1, 2, 3, 5, 8, 13, 21, 34, 55 etc.) named after the Italian scientist's findings of this numerical configuration in the natural world." (Flood & Morris 2001, p. 9) The main challenge is to think how "would be possible to use this work as a home?" (9) or, in other words, to think to what extent the traditional rationality of life and the rationality of number still can cohabitate in a capitalist age in order to let the individual to access a very natural lifestyle.

3 Merisa Merz's statement from the vernissage of her exhibition, including the work "Nylon threads" is revealing in this aspect: "There has never been any division between my life and my work." (Flood, Morris 2001, p. 5).

References

Bell, D., 1979, *Les Contradictions culturelles du capitalisme*, PUF, Paris.

Benjamin, W., 1968, *Illuminations: Essays and Reflections*, ed. by Hannah Arendt, trans. by Harry Zohn, Schocken Books, New York.

Boltanski, L. & Chiapello, E., 2005, *The New Spirit of Capitalism*, trans. by Gregory Elliott, Verso, London / New York.

Bourdon, D., 1995, *Warhol*, Abrams Inc., New York.

Ferry, L., 1977, *Homo Aestheticus*, Editura Meridiane, Bucureşti.

Ferry, L., 1993, *Homo Aestheticus. The Invention of Taste in the Democratic Age*, The University of Chicago Press, Chicago / London.

Flood, R. & Morris, F., 2001, *Zero to Infinity: Arte Povera 1962–1972*, TATE Modern, London, available at http://www.tate.org.uk/download/file/fid/6630, visited on July 20, 2021.

Hopkins, D., 2000, *After the Modern Art, 1945-2000*, Oxford University Press, Oxford.

Lipovetsky, G. & Serroy, J., 2013, *L'estethisation du monde. Vivre a l'age du capitalisme artiste*, Gallimard, Paris.

Fabro, Luciano, 2001, "On Marble and Silk", in *Catalogue "From Zero to Infinity: Arte Povera 1962–1972"*, Tate Modern Museum, available at https://www.tate.org.uk/search?q=From+Zero+to+Infinity%3A+Arte+Povera+1962%E2%80%931972, visited on December 12, 2021.

Marinetti, F. Th., 1909, "Manifeste du futurisme," in *Le Figaro*, Numéro 51, Gallica, Bibliothèque nationale de France.

Roger, A., 1995, *Art et anticipation*, Carré, Paris.

Rosenberg, H., 1972, *The De-Definition of Art*, The University of Chicago Press, Chicago / London.

Şerban, O., 2016a, *Artistic Capitalism. The Consumption of the Work-of-Art in Four Steps: Marcuse, Baudrillard, Debord and Lipovetsky*, Paralela 45, Piteşti.

Şerban, O., 2016b, "Why Is the De-Aestheticisation of Art a Phenomenon Specific to the Artistic Capitalism?," in *IJAPHC – The International Journal of Aesthetics and Philosophy of Culture*, Issue 1, No. 1/2016, pp. 87–102.

Online Source

Tate Modern Museum, "From Zero to Infinity: Arte Povera 1962–1972", 2001, available at https://www.tate.org.uk/documents/234/artepoveracards.pdf, visited on July 20, 2021.

6 Final Evaluation

6.1 Task

Write an original essay on the nature of the relationship between a certain form of cultural capital (deliberately chosen by you) and the human capital related to it. Follow the structure designs for research and content suggested in the following pages.

Please respect all the standards of professional deontology and academic integrity in order to produce an original paper.

6.2 Structure of the Research Design

6.2.1 Formal Requirements

- Minimum 8 pages, not including the title, abstract, keywords and bibliography.
- Abstract – maximum 10 lines. Specify the main objective of your research, the hypothesis involved in your research (briefly) and the (estimated results) conclusions reached at the end of your project.
- Keywords – between 5 and 8.
- Format: Times New Roman, 12; 1.5 lines; 0-0 spacing.
- Graphic elements and tables (if present) included in a separate document and not adding to the page number requirement.
- Structure your project proposal using sections in order to be clear for the evaluator what are the subject / theme of research, the objectives of the research, the working hypothesis, the state of the art, the synopsis of your contribution, the methodology involved, the estimated results, the confirmed results – final

DOI: 10.4324/9781003329855-7

conclusion, the bibliography and other annexed contents (see content structure).

Bibliography sorted alphabetically in the same document, with the references indicated in Chicago style: http://www.chicagomanualofstyle.org/tools_citationguide.html or APA (attached), on condition of consistency throughout the research plan (i.e. not mixing the two).

- References in text marked as footnotes or included in the text in between parentheses, if a Chicago style is chosen.
- Sections and subsections numbered as below.
- First page, top left corner – your name, MA programme and year.

6.3 Content Structure

6.3.1 General Requirements

a   Students are free to choose a form of ***cultural capital*** that they would like to investigate. There are no constraints related to the historical background or social dynamics of such form of cultural capital. Students are neither restricted to follow a specific institutional pattern assigned to the form of cultural capital selected for investigation throughout this research.

b   Students are required to:
   - Define the acceptance in which they use the notion of ***cultural capital*** and to present, extensively, the form of cultural capital selected for this critical analysis (genealogy, historical background, social implications, political implications if they are applicable).
   - Apply *Bourdieu's theory on the three stages of cultural capital* on the example chosen by them.
   - Evaluate how a such form of cultural capital is related to a certain level of ***performance*** that individuals achieve in a particular domain related to it.
   - Explain if there are any ***social inequalities*** generated by such a form of cultural capital within a specific group / community / society.
   - Analyze the connections between the selected form of cultural capital and the ***human***, respectively the ***social capital*** related to it.

- Identify the mechanisms of *social reproduction* specific to the type of cultural capital selected for their research.
- Explain the mechanisms of *creative communication* specific to the selected form of cultural capital that supports the social reproduction of the capital and develops the related human capital.
- Predict *the evolution* of such a form of cultural capital.

6.3.2 Design of Research

a **Cover page**

b **Title** of the research project. Students are encouraged to introduce a **subtitle** if their research leads to a certain **study case**.

c **Introduction**: identify the general area of study – if interdisciplinary, identify the disciplines intersecting; explain the motivation for having chosen the topic and its interest for the field of research. Apply the distinction between area of research and subject of research in order to narrow the path of your research. Explain how the interdisciplinary background of your research affects the hypotheses and the objectives selected for your research in terms of problems, conceptual gaps, innovation, and any other relevant factors.

d **State of the art and literature review**: emphasise the key points of how the topic has been discussed in the literature you have surveyed, what is the basic background information of the topic – identify whether there is an established debate (or various) to which you want to refer further, briefly present a few key points or studies that have been already done in this area; point out why it is necessary to continue exploring the topic: is there anything worth deepening or placing in another context, i.e. in a more interdisciplinary perspective? Refer to at least two state-of-the-art publications (most recent and relevant for the selected topic). Ensure exploration of the state of the art by paying equal attention to theoretical and practical content, and to common methodologies employed at the time when the literature to which you refer has been developed. The most important part is to explain how your research is going to bring something **new** into the scientific field (in terms of hypothesis, approach, results), overcoming the main gaps and problems raised by the selected literature (see Pickering 2008 for recommendations in what concerns the research design).

e   **Define one or two research problems**: questions that you want to investigate on your own; explain the context and the particular aspect you think is of interest for researchers. Make sure that you explain the connection between the scientific background (including the state of the art previously discussed) and the research problems.

f   **Define one or two research hypothesis/es**: make sure they can be applied. Suggest an explanation, a causal relation, an implication, a view that you may want to challenge. In other words, correlate the problem, the hypothesis and a projected / estimated result that might be obtained in the light of the hypothesis. Explain why a specific hypothesis can develop new approaches and appropriate tools to solve the problems identified at point d.

g   **Methods** used: explain the descriptive and interpretive components, conceptual and empirical. Make the distinction between qualitative and quantitative methods of research and explain where (in which part / section of the research) and why (depending on the hypotheses and estimated results) you choose one or another. Students are asked to explain, on the other hand, why their topic of research is more exposed to specific types of methods – qualitative and quantitative – and define possible constraints and consequences of this predetermination on the evolution of the research.

h   **Conclusion**: formulate the results you obtained or expect to obtain, how they contribute to solving the research problem(s) mentioned, the significance of the conclusion for the topic of your research. Indicate the most important achievements and the main gaps and vulnerable parts of your research. Include a short section devoted to **the openings of your research** (possible theoretical and practical paths to further develop the results obtained at the end of this project).

i   **Add the complete list of references** (books, journal papers, online resources). Ensure you apply a citation style from the list discussed at our research seminar.

j   If appropriate, **include (numbered) annexed contents** (tables, charts, questionnaires, interpretation of interviews or other materials that the student considers relevant for his project proposal).

6.4 Evaluation Scale

GENERAL REQUIREMENTS	MAX. 80 p.
2a	10 p
2b	10 p
2c	10 p
2d	10 p
2e	10 p
2f	10 p
2g	10 p
2h	10 p
DESIGN RESEARCH	MAX. 10 p.
1	10 p
2	10 p
3	10 p
4	10 p
5	10 p
6	10 p
7	10 p
8	10 p
9	10 p
10	10 p
FORMAL REQUIREMENTS	MAX. 10 p.

Figure 6.1 An evaluation scale to quantify the level of students' performance in what concerns both general requirements and design research standards.

References

Little, T. D. (ed.), 2013, *The Oxford Handbook of Quantitative Methods, Vol. 1. Foundations*, 1st ed., Oxford University Press, New York.

McLaren, M., 1998, *Interpreting Cultural Differences: Challenge of Intercultural Communication*, Dereham Peter Francis Publishers, Dereham, Norfolk.

Pickering, M. (ed.), 2008, *Research Methods in Cultural Studies: Research Methods for Cultural Studies*, 1st ed., Edinburgh University Press, Edinburgh.

Index